THE ANSWERS
The Best of TradingMarkets' Trading Advisor

Edited by Eddie Kwong

Lewis Borsellino
Mark Boucher
Larry Connors
Jeff Cooper
Daniel P. Delaney
Marc Dupee
Mark Etzkorn
Loren Fleckenstein
Kevin Haggerty
Mike Haran
Duke Heberlein
Jim Hyerczyk
Gary Kaltbaum
Tsutae Kamada
Greg Kuhn
Dave Landry
Kevin N. Marder
Sterling Ten

M. GORDON PUBLISHING GROUP
Los Angeles, California

ISBN: 1-893756-11-4

Printed in the United States of America

Disclaimer

It should not be assumed that the methods, techniques, or indicators presented in this book will be profitable or that they will not result in losses. Past results are not necessarily indicative of future results. Examples in this book are for educational purposes only. The author, publishing firm, and any affiliates assume no responsibility for your trading results. This is not a solicitation of any order to buy or sell.

The NFA requires us to state that "HYPOTHETICAL OR SIMULATED PERFORMANCE RESULTS HAVE CERTAIN INHERENT LIMITATIONS. UNLIKE AN ACTUAL PERFORMANCE RECORD, SIMULATED RESULTS DO NOT REPRESENT ACTUAL TRADING. ALSO, SINCE THE TRADES HAVE NOT ACTUALLY BEEN EXECUTED, THE RESULTS MAY HAVE UNDER- OR OVERCOMPENSATED FOR THE IMPACT, IF ANY, OF CERTAIN MARKET FACTORS, SUCH AS LACK OF LIQUIDITY. SIMULATED TRADING PROGRAMS IN GENERAL ARE ALSO SUBJECT TO THE FACT THAT THEY ARE DESIGNED WITH THE BENEFIT OF HINDSIGHT. NO REPRESENTATION IS BEING MADE THAT ANY ACCOUNT WILL OR IS LIKELY TO ACHIEVE PROFITS OF LOSSES SIMILAR TO THOSE SHOWN."

To Larry Connors
for his inspiration and unflagging
support over the years.

CONTENTS

GLOSSARY   183

RESOURCES/RELATED MATERIALS   195

ACKNOWLEDGMENTS

Thanks to Vincent Mao and Tsutae Kamada for helping me in the wee hours and on weekends to bring order to this project.

INTRODUCTION

All of us traders are on a mad hungry hunt for the Answers.

We want the Answers that will enable us to conquer the markets and become successful as traders.

There are many places to get answers from.

If you were to rank them in order of preference, starting with the most effective, I think it would come out something like this:

1. Getting one-on-one interactive instruction from a successful trader

2. Learn through seminars given by top traders

3. Have a way of listening to or reading the insights of top traders as they interpret and act upon market action each day

4. Read books and articles in which traders describe in detail their tools and strategies

5. Learn through trial and error (experience)

6. Learn from self-proclaimed "educators" who make a living teaching, but who actually don't themselves trade

The top 5% of all traders who are most single-mindedly determined to succeed and maximize their potential are likely to pursue all of these approaches (hopefully learning to avoid number 6), no matter what the cost in time and money.

Others may be just as obsessed about the idea of perfecting their trading skills, but may not be fortunate enough to receive guidance from these sources.

They would love to get all the benefits of one-on-one interactive instruction, seminars, daily insights, books, and experience somehow, some way in one convenient package—if they could.

The Answers is designed to meet their needs.

This book is an organized collection of all the very best questions and answers that have been published in "TradingMarkets' Trading Advisor"—a weekly feature of TradingMarkets.com. Through this feature, traders from different backgrounds trading in different time frames with different experience levels are able to ask questions and receive answers from the best and most consistently successful traders in the business.

In a very real sense *The Answers* is a compact version of all the most effective paths to learning rolled into one package. It's *Market Wizards* and *The Best*—but this time, instead of Jack Schwager or Kevin Marder asking the questions, it's regular traders like you and me interviewing the top traders.

Our problems, our struggles, and areas where we need fine-tuning are now addressed by professional traders.

And we have a big advantage here. We ask the questions that matter to *us*.

These are the questions that make a huge difference in our own trading performance. Not the questions that someone else thinks may be important to us. And yes—we even ask a few "dumb" questions that no professional interviewer would dare ask. But it's the willingness to ask "dumb" questions and soak in the answers that can make the difference between you blowing out your account every six months and becoming a trader who enjoys continual success for the rest of his life.

Every one of the traders answering the questions started somewhere. Likely in their early days, they made the same mistakes that all the rest of us make.

THE SELECTION PROCESS

In selecting the questions and answers that appear in this book, let me explain my approach.

I looked for answers that provided the knowledge, strategy or wisdom that is likely to improve the trading results of a wide cross-section of traders.

I was careful not to judge questions by how sophisticated the writer sounded or how intelligent the question was. After all, the questions we normally hesitate to raise our hands about, out of embarrassment, are often the ones that everybody wants to ask. These are the very ones that could be of profound benefit to many people.

I judged answers for substance—not style, grammar or length.

I let the traders be themselves so that you can hopefully feel their unique personalities rise off the written page. This is important. You want not only to understand strategies, but you also want to capture the feelings and attitudes of people that you want to become like. Some of the best gems in the book are short or "off the wall" answers.

ORGANIZING THE BOOK

Just as important as the information contained in this book is the way it is organized. I basically made a book that I would want to read. So, I focused much of my effort on sorting information logically so that you could not only find it easily, but also so that you might stumble across useful information serendipitously. As you might expect, the questions and answers didn't all fit neatly into one category. When necessary, I cross-referenced.

This is how I laid it out:

1. **Stock Selection.** This is one component of successful trading that is common to all trading styles. All daytraders, swing traders and intermediate-term traders go through a process of sorting through thousands of stocks every day to identify the best trading candidates.

2. **Trading Strategies.** In this section, we take a close look at the questions that people have about specific trading strategies. I define a strategy as a multi-step process that takes you through a trade from beginning to end.

3. **Intermediate-Term Trading.** You'll get the answers from top intermediate traders about nuances and techniques for finding stocks with the mix of fundamentals and technicals that portend runs lasting from weeks to months.

4. **Harnessing the Power of Momentum.** I was tempted to call this section "Swing Trading," as many of the questions are most relevant to traders who tend to hold positions for several days. But really, momentum plays a key role in successful trading for all time frames, particularly for the swing and daytrading time frames.

5. **Daytrading.** This section contains the questions and answers that specifically relate to the powerful strategies, tools and tricks used by traders for whom "hitting and running" is a way of life.

6. **Shorting**. I made this a separate category because successful shorting is much more than reversing long strategies. All traders experience the same challenges in shorting. Read how the Best handle them.

7. **Pattern Setups.** Most traders, myself included, think that much of what you need to know is contained in the price and volume action that is visible in a standard bar chart. In this section, the top traders will answer questions about their favorite patterns.

*Before you **dig into** **The Answers,** **there are a few important things I'd** **like to point out . . .***

- ***This is not a strategy instruction manual.*** *Outside of what I've done to put all the questions and answers into a logical, useful order, the content of this book has been dictated by traders like you and me. You will find that this book focuses on the knowledge gaps, challenges, sticking points and frustrations that traders face on a daily basis. Because traders are answering specific questions about strategies, patterns and other aspects of trading, you won't necessarily see an in-depth, step-by-step description of any one strategy. So, for example, if you want to learn everything you need to know about how to trade a Cooper 1-2-3-4 setup, it's best to go straight to the source and read Jeff's* Hit and Run *books.*

- ***I placed more emphasis on the answers than the questions.*** *In some cases, the questions have been edited down to allow more room in the book for answers.*

- ***You'll see different traders answering similar questions differently.*** *There is something of value to be learned from this. Realize that this is a reflection of the different styles among traders dealing in different time frames.*

- ***This is a book that is designed for use by all traders, regardless of whether they are members of TradingMarkets.com.*** *Because the questions in this book originally appeared in TradingMarkets.com, you will find that some of the questions mention our website. In no way does this dilute the usefulness of the answer to the general trading population.*

- ***I know it's obvious . . . but pay attention to the context of the question.*** *Many times someone will refer to the market at the time a question is being asked. The trader's answer will give a highly educational response, but also refer to the markets within a specific context. It's important for you to be aware of this in order to get the maximum benefit from the knowledge being handed to you.*

- ***The traders answering the questions avoid giving advice about stocks specifically asked about.*** From time to time, questioners will ask what they should do about a specific situation they are in with a given trade. While the trader answering the question may talk about the stock, their main mission is to educate. So you'll generally find that answers will focus on the larger issues that arise out of the situation described.

CHAPTER 1

Stock Selection

I *have met and had in-depth discussions with some of the most successful traders in the business. They are a diverse lot. They trade in different time frames (day-, swing-, and intermediate-term) and use dramatically different trading strategies.*

Still, they all tend to have two things in common.

- *They manage their money in such a way that losses are minimized, and gains are maximized.*

- *When the trading day ends, their workday is half over. They spend much of the rest of the waking hours in a process known as* **stock selection.**

Stock selection is roughly analogous to taking a level playing field and tilting it in your favor. Doing this is nothing more than putting together a list of the strongest stocks as a raw list of long candidates and a list of weakest stocks as a raw list for short candidates. You use these two lists as your starting point in identifying viable buy and sell candidates. The criteria used to build these lists vary depending on trading style. But typically, traders look at a mix of fundamentals and technicals:

Fundamentals: Earnings, revenues, products, industry leadership, institutional sponsorship, management, etc.

Technicals: Relative strength, momentum, trend strength, buy- and sell-side volume, patterns, new highs and lows, etc.

Changes in a company's fundamentals tend to fuel long-term shifts in its stock price.

Thus, shorter-term traders tend to emphasize the importance of technicals and pay less attention to fundamentals, whereas longer-term traders tend to pay close attention to both.

Once these lists are created, the trader will look more closely at each stock's patterns and technicals in search of trading setups.

WHY SPEND THE TIME?

Q: *One of my biggest problems in trading is being too overwhelmed with ideas from all directions. I have often thought I would be much better off focusing on a static list of good candidates, rather than trying to follow hundreds every night, but everyone seems to suggest that continually rotating your candidates is the only way to make money. Any thoughts or comments would be appreciated.*

Answered by Daniel P. Delaney 2000-03-11
It can be beneficial for a trader to remain focused on the same group of individual stocks because you can become familiar with their individual patterns and nuances. But you always have to remember that leadership rotates. What's hot today may be tomorrow's dog. Thus, you have to be willing to continually move to where the action is. Momentum trading demands that a trader follow the stocks that are moving and that have high-relative-strength indications, so you usually have to be open to new stocks all the time.

IN A BEAR MARKET

Q: *In a market like this where market leaders may have been trashed 40–50%, when is the best time to buy? If these stocks are blasting off when the new bull market starts, do you need to wait for new highs before buying again? When is the best time to buy these stocks after such declines in market leaders?*

Answered by Loren Fleckenstein 2001-01-13

If you trade the intermediate term, once you see the major indexes following through on strong volume, you can enter positions. As an intermediate-term momentum trader, I screen the market after each close looking for possible additions to my watch list. A stock does not have to make a new high to trigger a buy signal, but that is certainly a bullish event. I generally want my potential buys to have (1) retraced at least half of its correction (more is better); (2) cleared its 50- and 200-day moving averages; (3) have a 12- or six-month relative strength of 90 or higher; and (4) confirm the breakout with an RS nearing or breaking into new high ground on or before the price breakout. As for which watchlist stocks to buy and when, I buy them in order of breakout. In a really strong emerging rally, the number of valid breakouts will proliferate enough so that once I'm fully invested, there will still be breakouts occurring that I cannot take advantage of. As I get stopped out of the losers, I'll rotate that cash into other breakouts as they occur.

Q: *Is it helpful to monitor market laggards to see whether selling is intensifying in the similar-yet-opposite manner that we follow market leaders for signs of strengthening buying?*

Answered by Loren Fleckenstein 2000-12-23

For shortable stocks in down markets, I would look at stocks with very low relative strength and very poor earnings. However, for the most part, I trade long. I'm pretty asymmetrical in my trading; preferring to trade long in healthy markets and sit on cash in adverse markets. So I find little reason to screen for laggard stocks. I care about strong buying or strong selling in the leading, high-relative-strength stocks because those are the waters I fish in. Remember: It's a market of stocks, not a stock market. The market is really thousands of markets in different stocks. The issue is how the market is treating your quarry, not how it's treating the dozens or hundreds of other types of stocks out there that don't meet your screening criteria. What I need to know about the rest of the market, I can find out from the general averages and from looking each day at the stocks that moved up or down on heavy volume.

Q: *Assuming that the general market has established a definite uptrend and a particular industry is showing evidence of emerging leadership, how do I determine which particular stock is the true emerging leader of this particular industry group? Are fundamental considerations (e.g., growth rates, profitability) or technical considerations (e.g., cup-and-handle with a strong pre-existing uptrend and at least x% correction) most important in determining the price potential of a particular stock?*

Answered by Loren Fleckenstein 2000-11-11
Fundamental and technical considerations are both important. Your target stocks should have high-relative-strength and earnings growth. If you focus on a winning industry, the market will tell you which one to buy. Assuming you are looking at several high-performance stocks in the same industry, you buy them in order of breakout. The true leaders tend to break out of sound bases first as the market rallies from a bottom.

TECHNIQUE

Q: *In Gary Kaltbaum's commentary at the beginning of the week, he mentioned looking through 5000 charts over the course of the weekend. David Landry also mentioned once that he spends on average 3–5 seconds per chart. Although Gary's expertise lays in a different time frame from Landry's (i.e., intermediate-term vs. short-term), both of you obviously share the same skill—sizing up a chart in a very short period of time. How do you actually do it?*

Answered by Gary Kaltbaum 2000-12-30
After years of charting, it is now automatic. It's like looking in a photo album

for familiar faces. Over time, you get a feel for what looks good or bad—what's breaking down or out, or stocks setting up. It just takes time to get used to it. I always look at yearly charts, but also five-year charts as well. It is about recognizing certain patterns. The first thing I do is cross out charts that have no pattern to them. Secondly, I isolate stocks that are breaking down. This gives me a good idea about the market. The more stocks that break down, the worse the outlook I would have. I then look for setups that are basing and have a chance to break out. Lastly, for stocks that are breaking out, it's all about pattern recognition. Time will take care of you becoming faster at it. I remember when I spent hours each weekend looking at chart books. Now I run through them in 1–2 hours. Keep studying what a good chart looks like, as well as the bad, and keep at it. This is my best advice.

Q: *For Greg Kuhn: When there are so many potential great plays from terrific patterns, how do you choose which one or two to get into? Also, what is usually the best time of day for entry (e.g., is it at the morning open or some other time)?*

Answered by Greg Kuhn 2000-06-17
Go with the highest RS rank within a highly ranked group; with the highest percentage quarterly earnings growth; and with strong up-day volume surges as the stock completes the right side of its basing pattern. Best time of day for entry is *any* time, because valid breakouts occur throughout the trading day. Thanks for your question.

Q: *My biggest problem is finding the hottest sectors and groups, and then the stocks to focus on. For example, Kevin Marder, in one of his recent commentaries, said he was monitoring a watch list of 68 stocks. I would like to know how he arrived at his particular stocks. That is, what screens or web sites did he use to find the leading sectors and groups, and, ultimately, the 68 stocks? Could you expound on this?*

Answered by Kevin Marder 2000-06-24
There's no easy way to do this. To get a thorough look below the surface of the big averages, I look at a few thousand charts throughout the course of the

week. I look for three things, which I describe in the Kuhn/Marder course: high earnings growth expected over the next two years, high relative strength over the last eight weeks, and a sound basing pattern. As for the third criterion, I like to follow stocks that are more than just a step or two from completing their bases. Should a market take off in earnest to the upside, many stocks will complete the right sides of their patterns in haste. This is why it's important to include stocks whose price is more than just a percent or two away from their pivot.

Q: How much weight do you put on mutual fund ownership in the stocks that make up your watch list? Specifically, do you avoid stocks that have a percentage of fund ownership of more than 40% (as Mark Boucher does), even if they make the earnings and relative strength screens? This seems to make good sense, the logic being that if so many funds already have a large position in the stock, then who is left to push up the stock's price? In your experience, are the bigger winners those stocks that are yet undiscovered (for example, with a percentage of fund ownership less than, say, 15%)?

Answered by Greg Kuhn 2000-06-17
I have studied this extensively for several years and have found no level of fund-ownership percentage to be indicative of whether or not to avoid a stock. Therefore, I don't put any weight in that whatsoever.

Q: I see stocks that look like good buys from technical and fundamental points of view, but some of these stocks already have an institutional ownership of 80%. What can be considered in today's market as being over-owned by institutions? It seems to me that stocks with such high institutional ownership will have a hard time making substantial gains in a reasonable time.

Answered by Mark Boucher 2000-06-24
Stocks with high institutional sponsorship can still move quickly, but you're taking on more risk. We don't like high institutional sponsorship because the accumulation of a stock by an institution is one of the primary forces that allows the P/E multiple to expand rapidly. The ideal stock has an institutional

sponsorship of between 2% and 15%, with the trend in that sponsorship increasing. You're really looking for a rising trend in sponsorship from a relatively low level. That tells you that the elephants are herding into the stock. Once a stock has 35% to 40% institutional sponsorship, it is over-owned. It's already dominated by institutions. That substantially increases your risk level in the stock. If a stock with low institutional sponsorship misses its earnings estimate, it usually won't take as large a hit as a stock with high institutional sponsorship. When an over-owned company announces that earnings will be less than expected, it gets killed. Institutions, which watch earnings closely, dump it at the same time. You can make an exception, but you should have no more than one or two over-owned stocks in a six-stock portfolio.

Q: *I want to know if you think a short-term trader should only trade stocks that set up in the top two or three strongest sectors. It seems my best trades come from the stronger sectors, but I have this strange need to try and trade every "good" setup, no matter what sector the stock is in. Any insight?*

Answered by Dave Landry 2000-03-11
In general, you're better off sticking with the stocks in the strongest two or three sectors. This way, the "rising tide" will tend to lift all boats. So even if you don't pick the best stocks in the sector, your stocks may rise anyway. However, depending on how confident you are in picking stocks, you may occasionally want to consider stocks outside the strongest sectors. This may allow you to catch industry leaders in a soon-to-be-strong sector or niche stocks (i.e., at the time this is being published, fuel-cell stocks are very hot).

THE GENERALS

Q: *In his column, Mr. Haggerty makes several references to the "Generals." Can he please elaborate on the function of this group and their effect on the market?*

Answered by Kevin Haggerty 2000-01-22
The "Generals" are the giant institutions, mutual funds, banks and hedge

funds that manage billions of dollars in investment money. I call them the Generals because they have so much power and influence over our capital markets. For instance, if Fidelity Magellan decides to increase its holdings of a particular stock, that can translate into the purchase of millions of shares of a company. If a trader can monitor these Generals and understand how they can move the markets, by simply following the Generals, a trader can give himself a significant edge.

Q: *I want to learn more about how a large fund typically handles a breach of support in one of its major holdings. For example, let's say that Cisco sells off after some negative news, and it now has established support at 50. If 50 is broken, how would a major fund family respond:*

1. *Liquidate all or a portion of its position (in 1k, 10k, 100k, or whatever size chunks)?*

2. *Continue to hold the position because it's a core holding?*

3. *Sell a portion and re-buy lower as quickly as possible?*

As a small trader, I have a stop order just below 50. But if I'm stopped out, I would look to re-buy just above the next support level.

Answered by Kevin Haggerty 2000-06-03
Good question. Different managers will approach this differently, based on their evaluations of CSCO at these levels. You know, the "What price to pay for growth?" deal. No institution will just run in and blow out CSCO simply because it breaks 50. If the story is still good, you very well might see some more buying come in at the above levels, because of the valuation adjustment. I look at support levels and retracement levels as alerts in order to see what the generals will do. Remember: Elephants can't hide.

Q: *Kevin Haggerty, you pointed out in your seminar that many of the stocks overweighted by the Generals are in the S&P 500 and NDX and that these stocks enjoy the advantages of liquidity, tight spreads and "good average daily* *ranges." What do the Generals look for in terms of a stock's average daily range?*

Answered by Kevin Haggerty 2000-09-16
The Generals are looking at fundamentals in order to find their stocks. Good average daily ranges are something the Generals look to once they've zeroed in on a stock. Having a good average daily range is more of a trading tool than a trade indicator.

CHAPTER 2

Trading Strategies

A *trader who trades using a combination of chart patterns, price and volume action, and/or other technical tools and ties them together with a set of rules is using what is commonly called a trading strategy. Trading strategies vary in their complexity, but generally, the best ones are simple and include a loss-control component. There are a few things you should know about trading strategies:*

- *No one strategy is applicable to all trading environments and should never be traded blindly. Be sure to access the strength of the underlying trend of the market and individual industry groups.*

- *Losses are a part of the game and no one strategy should ever be traded without loss protection.*

- *All strategies should be used with discretion. The Holy Grail is a consistently profitable trading system that is 100% mechanical and makes all of your decisions for you. This does not exist. You must approach any strategy with an understanding of how it works, why it works, and under what circumstances it will work.*

- *Simple is best.*

TURTLE SOUP PLUS ONE

Editor's note: Some of the questions within the "Turtle Soup Plus One" section talk about futures. If you're a stock trader, please be aware that this strategy is equally applicable to stocks.

Q: *I have heard about Richard Dennis and his Turtles many times and have gathered that it is a breakout system. I have heard your site refer to certain setups as Turtle Plus One (or something like it), but I have never actually come across the exact specifics of these setups or systems. Can you explain it to me?*

Answered by Duke Heberlein 2000-08-26

The Turtles system employs breakouts from a 20-day high (or low). It tends to have periods of very large drawdowns and a low win-to-loss ratio due to the number of false breakouts that occur. The Turtle Soup and Turtle Soup Plus One setups attempt to take advantage of these false breakouts, in effect, doing the opposite of the turtle systems.

The rules for buys are (sells are reversed): 1) The stock must make a new 20-day low. 2) The previous 20-day low must have occurred at least four days earlier. 3) When the market falls under the prior 20-day low, you will enter 1/8 above the previous 20-day low. The Turtle Soup Plus One rules are the same. Your entry point is just one day later.

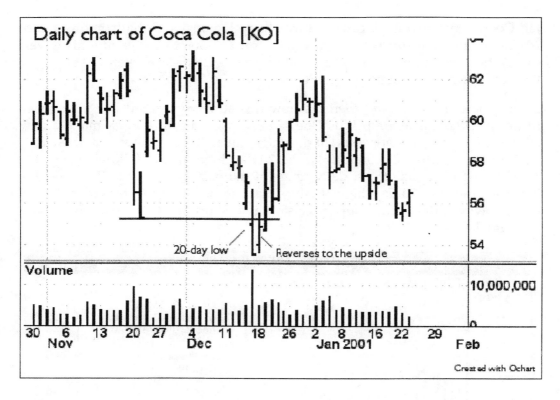

Daily chart of Coca Cola [KO]

20-day low

Reverses to the upside

Volume

10,000,000

30   6   13   20   27   4   11   18   26   2   8   16   22   29
     Nov   Dec   Jan 2001   Feb

Created with Ochart

Q: *Regarding the Turtle Soup Plus One strategy, are there other indicators that should be looked at that would help to pick out the strongest setups, or do you just trade every setup across the board? Please let me know if there is something else that would help to narrow the field.*

Answered by Marc Dupée 1999-05-22
Look at other indicators in the same futures group for clues. Soybean meal (SMN9) registered a Turtle Soup Plus One sell signal on Thursday, May 20. Soybeans (SN9) and soybean oil (BON9) had been on the Implosion-5 List and had been showing weakness by hitting 10-day and 20-day lows without reversing.

Jeff Cooper has a strategy called "Turtle Soup Expansions" that combines false 20-day Turtle Soup breakouts with range expansions to better identify reversals. When traders get squeezed on the wrong side of a market, the short- or long-covering rally can be powerful.

Let's review the rules and then see how this strategy worked out in soybean meal. Just like Turtle Soup Plus One sell setups, the future must make a new 20-day high and the previous 20-day high must have occurred at least four trading days earlier. On the day of the 20-day high, or the following day, the future must make its largest daily range of the past four days and reverse below the previous 20-day high. Rather than go short at the previous 20-day high, however, the Turtle Soup expansion goes short one tick below the expansion-day low.

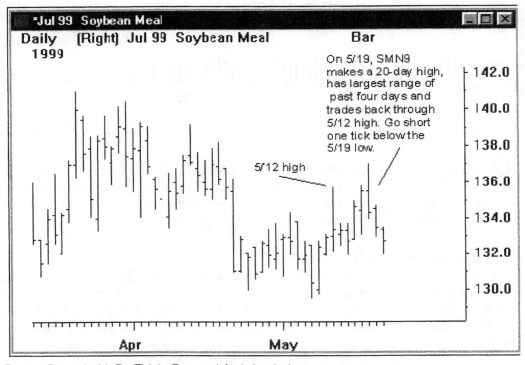

Source: Created with RealTick by Townsend Analytics, Ltd.

Q: *Concerning the Turtle Soup Plus One setups, are these reversals usually thought to be short-term if the commodity doesn't simultaneously appear on the momentum/implosion list? Are they more often true reversals or corrections/retracements of longer underlying trends?*

Answered by Eddie Kwong 2000-07-01

TS+1 can be longer or shorter term. Longer-term moves are more likely to occur after a strong trend has a long run and loses momentum. Intermediate-term trends are more likely to be of shorter duration. Cocoa, Natural Gas and Lean Hogs have all registered short-term Turtle Soup Plus One reversal signals. But at the same time, longer-term reversals have been in gold, coffee and interest rate futures.

Q: *Hi, Marc! Jeff Cooper mentioned that the June S&P futures (SPM0) gave a Turtle Soup Sell signal yesterday in reaction to the Fed's interest rate increase. What does he mean? Is he using it in an intraday context or based on the daily data? I don't understand what he is trying to say.*

Answered by Marc Dupée 2000-05-27

For the benefit of our readers, I would like to share our private e-mail correspondence on your question about Jeff Cooper's commentary and Turtle Soup Reversals. Here it is as follows:

In his "Momentum Stocks Insight," Jeff is referring to an intraday Turtle Soup Sell signal in the June S&Ps. Cooper sometimes looks at 10-minute intraday charts.

> *I didn't realize that the Turtle Soup setup could be successfully applied to intraday charts. Interesting idea!*

We see this a lot in the S&Ps: Turtle Soups (and TS+1s) on intraday charts. Vs occur often on the intraday Nasdaq 100 futures.

> *Interesting. What is the best way to set up a chart to spot the Turtle Soup signals? I use TradeStation. Any thoughts? And where is the best place to read about them?*

Just set your signals for a 20-day high. You will have to create a filter (or do it visually) where the previous 20-day high has not occurred within the past four days. Read about Turtle Soup Plus One setups on the Futures Indicators page.

We screen daily for both buy and sell setups for futures, although there are no signals for Wednesday. Turtle Soup setups trigger on the same bar that a 20-day high issues a false breakout (rather than the following bar, as in the Turtle Soup Plus One). You can also read about TS setups in the Connors and Raschke book *Street Smarts*.

Q: *I am a bit confused about the Turtle Soup signals. You mentioned that Cooper looks at 10-minute charts for intraday Turtle Soup signals. Does that mean that you look back for 20 10-minute bars (i.e., for 200 minutes) and look for a new high that did not occur within the last four 10-minute bars for a setup, or do you look at **20 days** instead?*

Answered by Marc Dupée 2000-05-27
You have it right. Cooper's look back was 20 10-minute bars. And that is what I meant in reference to the patterns we see in the S&Ps. If you're using five-minute bars, then it's 20 five-minute bars; if 10 minutes, then 20 10-minute bars, etc.

As you look at these, you'll notice that, like in all trading patterns, the "20-period" is not a scientific number. It can happen in 17 or 24. The principle is that a (approximate) 20-period extreme has been made and then a fake-out punch-through—without follow-through—occurs, signaling a reversal.

Q: *I see in the futures section that you have "Turtle Soup Plus One buy and sell setups." Can they be used for stocks, too? Are the rules and method the same?*

Answered by Marc Dupée 1999-05-01
The Turtle Soup Plus One method is designed specifically to take advantage of false breakouts and can be applied to stocks just as readily as futures contracts. Here are the rules: For a buy setup, a market must make a new 20-day low

and its previous 20-day low must have been made three or more days ago. You would go long the next day if the market trades above the low of the earlier 20-day low (indicating yesterday's 20-day low was a false breakdown). For sell signals, reverse the rules. Protective stops are placed at the recent (yesterday's) 20-day low for buys, or at the recent 20-day high for sells.

Here are some recent setups (both long and short) in AES.

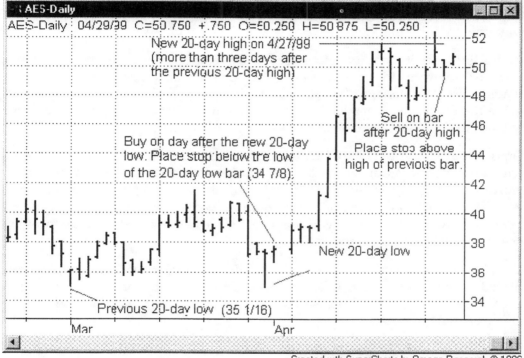

TRADING OFF NEWS

Q: *Should a daytrader use stocks in the news to trade? Many professional traders like to trade stocks that have no news because there is no "crowd congestion," and thus, it's very clear to see the "real" movement of the stock.*

Answered by Marc Dupée 1999-05-08

News events can cause a great deal of confusing "noise" in the markets, but trading stocks in the news is an excellent strategy, although perhaps not in the way you are thinking.

At TradingMarkets.com, we often use news events as contrarian indicators. If a stock or a future does not behave as a news event suggests it would, this sends a strong message that something is wrong and that the market will move the other way. Let's look at a news event this week that provided a nice contrarian short-sale opportunity.

On Tuesday, May 4, 1999, Cisco (CSCO) announced a deal to supply NASA with networking products for a new high-performance, wide-area computer network. A big government contract is bullish news, yet the stock sold off. Why? It is hard to be certain, but it could be because specialists sold into the hype. Whatever the reason, you want to find a low-risk entry point to be on board for the contrarian move.

To take advantage of the ostensibly "bullish" Cisco news, you could have placed a sell order one tick below the high of the day preceding the news event (just below 114 in this case). Risk no more than 1 point. Cisco sold off to 105 over two days.

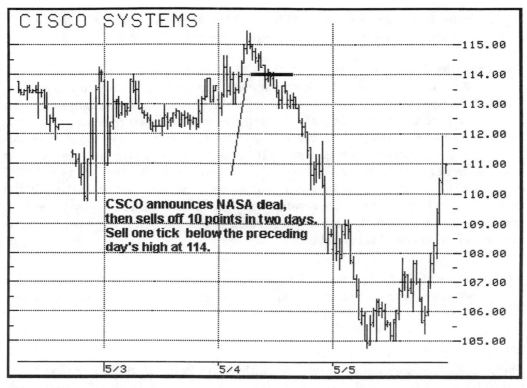

CISCO SYSTEMS

CSCO announces NASA deal,
then sells off 10 points in two days.
Sell one tick below the preceding
day's high at 114.

5/3   5/4   5/5

Source: Quote.com

Q: *At what point should you buy a stock after the company has announced a split and the deadline date? There are stocks I'm interested in and want to buy them at the correct point to have the most advantage.*

Answered by Tsutae Kamada 2000-11-25
According to Kevin Haggerty, "Splits are a non-event for institutions, and they often sell into the price advance." His advice is: "After a split selloff, you look for the same patterns you do every day."

Q: *I have a very direct question. What book or source teaches an individual trader to "read between the lines" of a company's press statement?*

Answered by Daniel P. Delaney 2000-03-25

While I do not know of any book that specifically teaches what you are asking, I would suggest you remain skeptical regarding press releases. Large companies like GE or Cisco are generally straightforward in press releases, but some caution should be used in interpreting newer or smaller companies. For example, once the Business-to-Business (B2B) theme became big, it seemed that many Internet companies suddenly started referring to themselves as a "B2B" company or talking about their B2B initiatives. This also happened with the term "Internet incubator." Be careful of those thinly traded companies that suddenly rise after a well-written press release. Remember, if something seems "too good to be true," it probably is.

Q: *I get really pissed off that I can't jump in early on IPOs. How can a small guy get in on these without buying at the highs after it goes public and watching it snap-back for a loss?*

Answered by Marc Dupée 1999-05-15

The following strategy might help by getting you in on an IPO after that initial "snap-back." It is a simple approach, and you can find additional chart examples in our book *The TradingMarkets.com Guide to Conquering the Trading Markets* in the section on Hot IPO Pullbacks.

First, you identify a company that has traded at least 15% higher within five days of going public. This helps filter out IPOs that aren't moving. So if an issue is priced at 15, it must trade to 17 1/4 in its first five days to be a candidate. Next, wait for a two- to four-day pullback. Then, between the second and fourth day of the pullback, buy 1/16 point above the high of the previous day and put your stop at that day's low. Hold the trade up to five days using, of course, trailing stops. For example, Bottomline Technologies (EPAY) goes public at $19 on 2/12/99, and trades at least 15% higher. After a four-day pullback, buy 1/16 above previous day's (2/19) high of 20 1/2. EPAY trades as high as 98 within three weeks.

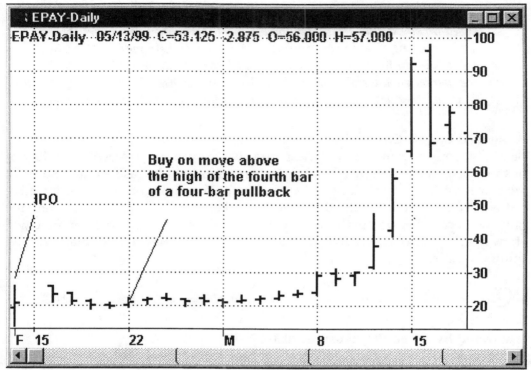

PUTTING IT ALL TOGETHER

Editor's Note: For some of the best traders in the world, the best system is no system at all. A trader like Jeff Cooper faces the market each day armed with a collection of indicators, patterns and tactics which he uses interchangeably depending on specific situations he runs across. Every day it's a custom-tailored "new system" that his mind instantly pieces together in order to fully exploit the new opportunities that arise.

Q: Mr. Cooper, I try to ride short-term rallies or declines for one to two days. I only enter a trade when a stock goes above/below a certain target price, which usually indicates that it will continue in that direction. Last week, I only focused on stocks that I expected to fall, and I lost money in all these trades. I am wondering if you know any clues which might help me identify when a stock is likely to reverse intraday so that I don't trade them. Would looking at the market advancers/decliners ratio 5–7 minutes after the open give me a hint as to whether advancers or decliners are likely to do such intraday reversals?

Answered by Jeff Cooper 2000-10-14

Basically, your best indicator is your two eyes. You must observe the behavior of the stock, and when you have paper profits on stocks, use trailing stops to lock in the profit. Don't let profits evaporate. You must observe the intraday pattern in conjunction with the overall market in individual stocks, and the only way you can do this is with your eyes. There is no indicator that will show you at the open what will happen later in the day. In the market, anything can happen.

Q: *Can someone comment (i.e., give a technical opinion) on the stock IDTC?*

Answered by Loren Fleckenstein 2000-02-19

As of Wednesday's close, IDTC was consolidating nicely after surging from Friday's close of 22 5/16 to 29 1/5. Ideally, you'd like to see the stock drift slightly lower, while the trading range contracts and volume abates, as it digests its gains, before it attempts to make another move to the upside, if it does so. If we set aside current general market conditions, you could set your buy point at the top of the consolidation range, buying if the stock breaks above that ceiling on strong volume. But make sure you set a price-stop that will get you out of the stock if it reverses on you. Keep your losses small! Going back to IDTC, the stock's last resistance ceiling was at 30, another pivot point, and its 52-week high, 35, constitutes another. The stock has a 12-month relative strength score of 81 and a six-month RS of 78. In other words, it has outperformed 81% and 78% of all other stocks in the TradingMarkets database over those time frames. So that's a nice show of strength.

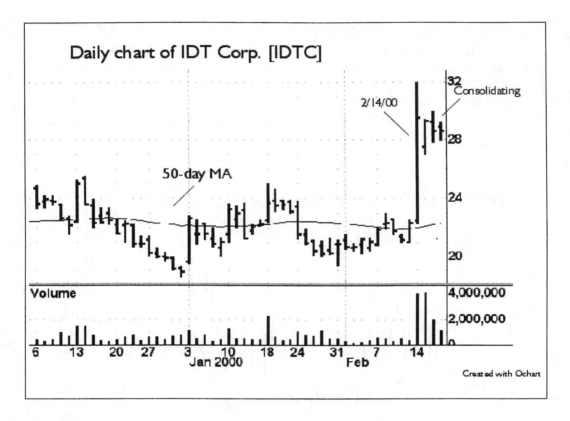

Daily chart of IDT Corp. [IDTC]

2/14/00

32
Consolidating

50-day MA

28

24

20

Volume

4,000,000

2,000,000

6   13   20   27   3   10   18   24   31   7   14
                        Jan 2000   Feb

Created with Ochart

Q: *On Jan. 27, someone on TradersWire, as well as Kevin N. Marder, made a comment about APNT forming a handle in the cup-and-handle pattern. I looked at the chart with interest at the time and purchased APNT at $56 per share. Within the next two or three days it went down to $46.00. It then started to climb back up. I bailed on the stock at $51.25 on 2/4/00. The stock then languished in the $49–54 range for the next couple of days. On the Feb. 10, APNT came out with great earnings and the stock that day went to $71. On Feb. 11, the stock came back to the low 60s. What a great trade I would have had if I had stayed in. What did I miss in looking at the chart? Where did I go wrong? At what price should I have placed the order on Jan. 27 and with the following downturn of the stock? Hindsight is great.*

Answered by Dave Landry 2000-02-19

Let's pick this trade apart, with hindsight of course! One can't argue with the pattern. It was there. But should this trade have even been taken in the first place? Notice that on Jan. 27 (a) the stock closed poorly and never rallied past the prior day's high (b). This suggested that the stock went weak and the pattern hasn't "proved" itself. So by waiting for stocks to re-assert themselves, you'll often avoid patterns that fail.

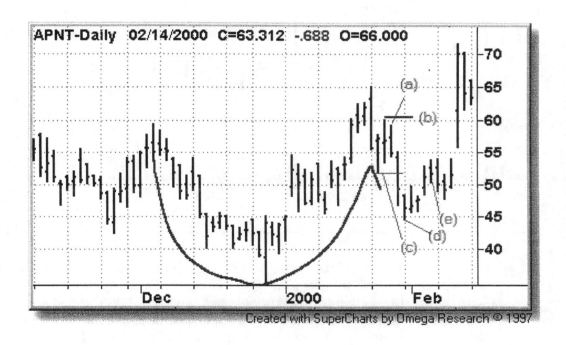

OK, so you took the trade. Let's deal with the management of it. I have three articles on the site on this subject. Mark Boucher has also written on this subject. So it's tough to be that comprehensive in this forum. With that said, the bottom of the handle would probably have been a good place for a protective stop (c). After all, the reason you got in the trade (cup-and-handle) may no longer be valid at this point. This would have protected your capital by letting you off the hook with a small loss and, what people often forget, allows you to focus on the next stock, which may have potential.

So you didn't get out there. You rode the stock all the way down to 44 3/4 (d). This means that the stock dropped over 20% since you bought it. Assuming you are a relatively short-term trader, this is way too much to risk on a trade. If you risked this much on every trade, assuming you're an active trader, it wouldn't take too long to wipe out an account.

OK, so you rode it down all the way to 44 3/4. You then sold the stock at (e). Now keep in mind that this is NOT saying you should hold on to bad trades (you should have been out at (c) as described above), but you did. And at this juncture, the stock was beginning to rally. Many people in bad trades often have the "I'll get out at break-even" mentality and either lose a tremendous amount of money as the stock continues to slide or, at the first sign of strength, get out and get completely frustrated as the strength continues. Here, you've done the latter.

Q: *I am impressed by the no-nonsense, businesslike manner of your site. I would like to suggest that you follow up on indicator leads that do not pan out and help us understand how this fits into technical analysis. Ann Taylor, for example, was listed for several days as a potential cup-and-handle, but has disappeared from the list. I notice that it has not gone down—in fact, it seems to be consolidating. What are the implications of this? I am sure you have other cases where stocks don't fit the patterns you think they will; fine, nothing is perfect, but we can learn from what doesn't work, too.*

Answered by Dave Landry 1999-10-16
Just like the fisherman who knows that in order to catch fish he must fish when the tide is moving, we as traders must seek out the best patterns and those markets that are likely to move. In the "Stock Market Trading Outlook," this is exactly what I do. If on subsequent days the stocks still look like they have potential, I'll continue to mention them. After several days of no action, I tend to drop these stocks out of the Outlook in favor of those that look like they have more potential for the following day.

The Ann Taylor (ANN) example you refer to did not pan out. This does not mean such stocks are not worth watching going forward. Often, the market will go where a bullish (or bearish) pattern suggests, but in many cases not right away. In other words, the market doesn't always give immediate gratification. For instance, Amazon was recently on our cup-and-handle list. The pattern (a) looked great to me but the stock then proceeded to trade sideways (b). When everyone "forgot" about the stock, it then exploded (c).

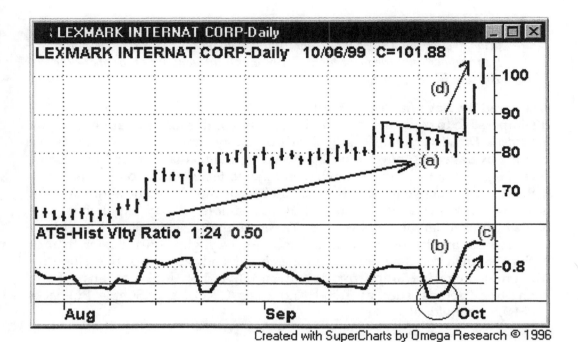

LEXMARK INTERNAT CORP-Daily

LEXMARK INTERNAT CORP-Daily 10/06/99 C=101.88

ATS-Hist Vlty Ratio 1.24 0.50

Created with SuperCharts by Omega Research © 1996

Lexmark (LXK) provides another great example. I mentioned it in my Trading Outlook (a) as a potential volatility explosion play (b) to the upside, but the stock continued to trade sideways. After several days the stock finally exploded (d), as volatility reverted to its mean.

To sum up: Yes, stocks that exhibit bullish (or bearish) patterns are definitely worth watching going forward, even if they don't move immediately. If a stock begins to sell off from a bullish pattern (or rally from a bearish pattern), you probably should remove it from your screens. However, as long as it doesn't do anything "wrong," it may be worth watching, provided it doesn't distract you from stocks that appear to have greater immediate potential.

Q: *When swing trading, what criteria would you suggest for the index (Nasdaq) prior to entering a stock long? For example, do you wait for the Nasdaq to trade higher than the prior high, just be on an intraday trend, be above the 200-day EMA, or what?*

Answered by Dave Landry 2000-10-07

It's impossible to cover my entire index analysis in this forum, but I'll give you a *Reader's Digest* version. I first look at the 50-day simple and 200-day simple moving averages, as they are well watched by the media. Unless I have some sort of signal (more on this below), then I like to focus mostly on the long side if the market is above these averages, and I focus mostly on the short side if it is below these averages. I also plot 10-day simple, 20-day exponential and 30-day exponential moving averages. These are the same averages I use in my Bow Ties setups. In these averages, I look for Daylight (lows greater than or highs less than for downtrends), proper order and slope (positive slope for uptrends, negative slope for downtrends). I then look for any of my swing-trade setups, such as Trend Knockouts (TKOs) and Simple Pullbacks (SPMs), in individual stocks.

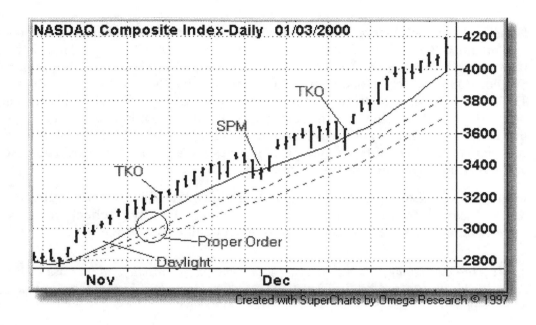

Created with SuperCharts by Omega Research © 1997

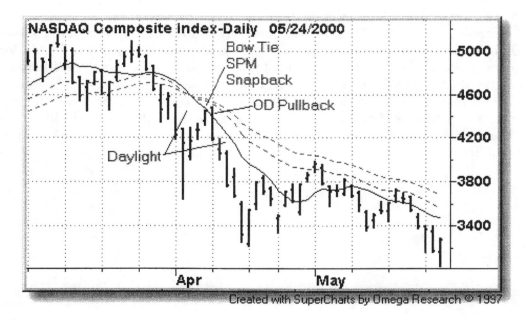

Created with SuperCharts by Omega Research © 1997

I also look at stock market indicators, such as the advances/declines and average of those (CHADTP). I make sure to study the VIX/CVR Signals and the three-period average of the TRIN indicator. I also have an Oscillator Swing System (OSS), which I follow (but do not trade directly) on the S&P futures. The system signals a potential buy signal (oversold) after five consecutive down days in the oscillator (a three-day moving average minus a 10-day moving average, essentially an MACD) and a sell signal (overbought) after five consecutive up days in the oscillator. This gives me a good idea of overbought and oversold, especially in choppy markets.

In addition to the above, I'll also look for recent highs/lows of the indices to see if I can determine support and resistance. Finally, I check for any late-breaking news that could throw a wrench in all of the above.

 To Dave Landry: I am wondering if you ever use Moneyflow to increase your odds on cup-and-handle formation breakouts. Have there been any studies on this?

Answered by Dave Landry 2000-05-20
Personally, I don't use Moneyflow. However, you may have discovered something indirectly. Normally, by combining signals, you increase your odds for success. For instance, the CVR I signal that corresponds with a CVR III signal on the Market Bias Page tends to lead to more reliable (i.e., higher-probability) signals than stand-alone signals. Therefore, by combining patterns (in this case, a cup-and-handle) with another stand-alone indicator, you will likely increase your odds of success (provided, of course, that the stand-alone indicator is robust).

CHAPTER 3

Intermediate-Term Trading

Popularized by William O'Neil, intermediate-term trading is one of the fastest-growing segments of the trading population. This methodology favors stocks that have a combination of a favorable business outlook and good technicals. Profitable trades typically last from weeks to months and trailing stops are moved higher to lock in profits. During bull markets, a proper execution of this approach can yield phenomenal results. However, players in this arena generally trade only on the long side and usually avoid shorts. Unless they're deviating from orthodoxy, they're going to be in cash during bear markets.

Q: *I would like your feedback on the O'Neil follow-through-day percentage. With the Dow in the 10,000 to 11,000 range and the Nasdaq in the 3,300 range, do you really think the follow-through percentage of 1% or more is realistic? Considering the volatility in the market and individual stocks, it is not uncommon to see one or more of the major averages fluctuate 1% or more several times a week. With this in mind, do you think the follow-through percentage should be raised to possibly 2% or 3%, at a minimum, to reflect a more accurate assessment of a potential follow-through?*

Answered by Greg Kuhn 2000-06-10

This has become an issue only in the last six months because up until the end of the fourth quarter of last year, we hadn't seen this level of volatility. The bottom line is that right now it's a lot easier to get the 1% moves, especially in the Nasdaq. However, the more important component to the follow-through-day system is actually seeing leading growth stocks breaking out of sound basing patterns. So, if you get a follow-through day, and if you see a number of high-quality, leading growth stocks breaking out of multi-week or multi-month basing patterns, then I think you take the signal. But when the 1% is taken alone, I can understand your question. Outside of just the signal, you really need those stocks breaking out of bases in tandem with the 1% moves.

Q: *You recently mentioned Rare Medium in your column. How can you consider a stock with such a low EPS ranking?*

Answered by Greg Kuhn 2000-02-26

Most of the Internet stocks, such as Rare Medium, do not have earnings. People buy them in anticipation of future earnings. Instead of looking at EPS, you should focus on revenue growth. Look for stocks with accelerating revenue growth. Three quarters ago, Rare Medium's revenue growth was 406%; two quarters ago it was 646%; and last quarter it was 719%, from a year ago. A general guideline is that for the stocks in the growth sectors such as Biotech, Telecommunications and Internet, do not focus on their earnings (EPS); instead, look for the ones with high relative strength and good chart patterns.

Q: *Referring to your comments after the close on Friday, Sept. 22, I don't understand your calling that day an accumulation day. The Naz index closed down, there were 400 more declining stocks than advancing stocks, and down volume was 50% greater than up volume.*

Answered by Kevin Marder 2000-09-30

In determining accumulation/distribution, I only look at days in which total volume was higher than that of the prior day. If price was up on such a day, it's accumulation. The opposite is true for distribution.

Friday, Sept. 22, 2000, was a close call. The Nasdaq did close lower. However, the fact that the index hit a low less than an hour into the day and spent the rest of the day rising, coupled with its wide-range bar and the fact that it was the heaviest-volume day in five months, told me it was more of an accumulation day than otherwise. That said, this is a fine line and can be interpreted in different ways by different people. Thus, there is no right way, only the way that makes the most sense to you.

Q: *For Loren Fleckenstein: You have been cautious toward this market, and it looks like you were right for being that way. I took a trade on NTAP when it hit its pivot point and got stopped out. Are you looking at overall market dynamics for a clue? The individual setups lately look inviting and then give it up, just leaving a higher pivot for the next time around.*

Answered by Loren Fleckenstein 2000-10-28
First, a caveat: My intermediate-term momentum-trading strategy departs somewhat from William O'Neil's CANSLIM, although I shoot for much the same in stocks—high 12-month relative strength, high earnings growth (in most cases, though not all), accumulation by institutions—under similar conditions (stocks breaking out from sound bases with positive indications on the major indexes and underlying market volume). To help confirm a new rally, I rely on O'Neil's follow-through day. With that caveat, I would not be buying in the current market. We have not had many follow-through days. And even if we get the FTD, I would not buy until I see a higher number of high-RS, high-EPS stocks forming nearly complete bases of, at bare minimum, five weeks in length and/or breaking out of sound bases. I am seeing very few of these kinds of stocks setting up in proper bases.

As you have observed yourself, the few that have emerged through pivot points have subsequently failed, or they have other problems, such as highly extended runs just prior to passing the pivot, which makes the stock vulnerable to profit-taking and pullbacks. For another example, see my Oct. 24 "Trading The News" analysis on Techne Corp. Your best indicator is the trading behavior of stocks meeting your buy requirements. If, as you seem to observe just as I have, there are relatively few proper-looking setups, and those few are failing, that tells you that the character of the market is unfavorable to your type of trading. In such conditions, stay in cash, wait for the market to provide evidence of a nascent rally by (1) giving you the FTD and (2) supplying you with a proliferation of high-quality stocks (high-earnings-growth, high-relative-strength) setting up in sound bases. Don't be tempted by the isolated base. You want to see a clear multiplication of basing stocks meeting your buy criteria. At true market bottoms giving birth to sustainable rallies, they come out of the woodwork *en masse*.

Q: *I have attempted trading twice before with less-than-stellar results, but thanks to hard knocks and, more recently, instruction from your site, I am having the best results I've ever had. If you can answer a question, I would appreciate it: I own TECH, CHKP, ANEN, ELNT, TLGD and NVDA. Today I experienced distribution in four of the six. One could view the NASDAQ today as churning. With relatively small profits in a short time period, what do you do? Try to ride out the first pullback?*

Answered by Kevin Marder 2000-07-01

As an intermediate-term trader, I strive to sit through the FIRST pullback in a leader in a new market advance. That's what the intermediate-term game is all about—holding stocks for substantial gains over a period of months. I do this because stocks such as these often go on to pile up some of the fattest gains in the ensuing market run. Buying a stock as it emerges from a well-formed base on big volume is the key here, since buying an extended stock will often whip you out of your position as it pulls back. In a fresh market advance, one distribution day in a stock isn't enough to worry me.

BREAKOUTS *(See also, MOMENTUM BREAKOUTS, page 69)*

From Long Bases

Q: *CCMP moved out of a flat base recently. The stock has great fundamentals and great technicals. The parent company will be selling the additional 80% of*

CCMP soon, after the lock-up period, I suppose. Will that flood the market with too many shares? Any comments on the rather short four-week base?

Answered by Loren Fleckenstein 2000-09-02
To my eye, anything shorter than six weeks is not a base.

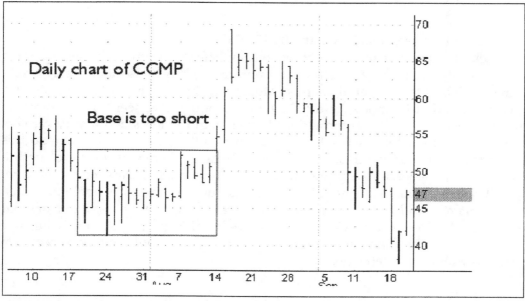

Source: Qchart.

This does not mean that such structures are not tradable, but they are riskier for the intermediate-term trade. At TradingMarkets, we don't make recommendations on individual stocks. However, I think you are wise to be wary of stepping in front of such an overhang. As you may know, TM's TradersWire issues an alert called "Triple 9s" to notify premium subscribers of heavy supply or demand coming to market. Sometimes, a big block of stock for sale takes time to work through the market, and the current market price may not fully discount that eventual selling. Once the supply is out of the way, a stock can rebuild its base.

Q: *How long must a stock's base be for its subsequent breakout to be significant? With respect to a cup-and-handle chart formation, if the right-hand side of the cup is significantly (maybe as much as 20%) higher than the left side, and if the handle is higher than the cup, would you consider the basing period to be just the handle formation or both the cup and the handle? If the last question sounds weird, have a look at two- and three-month charts of AMAT, KLAC, LSCC, LSI, MOT and TER.*

Answered by Loren Fleckenstein 2000-02-05

A stock should base for at least six weeks before it's properly set up for a meaningful breakout. This is the bare minimum. Mostly, sound basing structures will last far longer than this. Moreover, the better stocks will show a prior uptrend of least 30% before the base. Although I've seen stocks complete the right side of their cup formations higher than the left side on very rare occasions and then form what I call a "high handle," most stocks that do this carry faulty price structures. They're faulty because there was too much enthusiasm for the stock at the point where it really should've run into some light profit-taking, a.k.a.—the handle. The stock just became too obvious to too many players and will have a higher degree of "whipping" you out of your position. But I've seen stocks with these so-called high handles and what I've found is that the high on the right side of the cup shouldn't be more than 10%–15% above the left side.

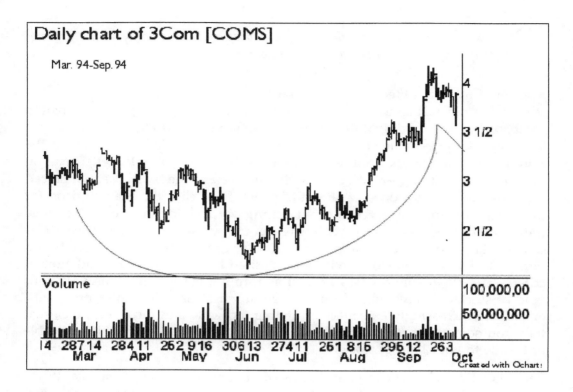

Daily chart of 3Com [COMS]

Mar. 94-Sep. 94

Volume

| 4
| 3 1/2
| 3
| 2 1/2

100,000,00
50,000,000

14 28 7 14 28 4 11 25 2 9 16 30 6 13 27 4 11 25 1 8 15 29 5 12 26 3
Mar   Apr   May   Jun   Jul   Aug   Sep   Oct

Created with Ochart!

That should be your rule-of-thumb. If you can, check out the cup-and-"high"-handle formation on Pre-Paid Legal Services (PPD) between January and April 1996 and 3Com (COMS) between March and September 1994. PPD completed the right side of its cup 15% above the left side, and COMS finished its cup 8% higher. Consider the whole formation—cup-and-high-handle—in your base count. Bear in mind, some smaller stocks will never form a handle and just blast right out of their cup formations. It can get tricky. But if you misjudge one that you're not quite sure about, there will be other stocks with unmistakable cup-and-handle formations in a good market environment. William O'Neil's study of history's greatest winning stocks shows that 80% of all big winners have emerged from the more traditional cup-and-handle. As for AMAT, KLAC, LSCC, LSI and MOT, they all just emerged from basic basing patterns.

Q: *I would like to know exactly how you go about finding a list of stocks forming fairly long (two- to five-month) very tight bases.*

Answered by Loren Fleckenstein 2000-02-19

Maybe I'm old fashioned, but I believe the best way is using your eyeball, a database like the TradingMarkets.com Stock Scanner and charts. First, screen for stocks with desirable criteria. Then pull up the chart for each stock on the resulting list and work your way down the list. For example, let's say you trade breakouts in high-relative-strength issues. Have the Stock Scanner screen for stocks with, say, a one-year RS of 85 to 99. Then click the charting icon for each stock on the list. I recommend setting your chart for a one-year time frame. From there, just work your way through until you have located those stocks that appear to be forming your kind of bases. I believe it's just as important to know when stocks with your desired technical and/or fundamental criteria are *not* in sound bases as well as forming constructive bases. If your kind of stocks are breaking down in large numbers or failing after breakouts, or looking increasingly extended, or getting too wide and loose, etc., etc., that tells you something important about whether the overall market is favorable or hostile to your kind of stocks.

Each day, I review the charts of dozens of high-relative-strength stocks. When the market is bottoming after a correction, scads of high-RS stocks will complete sound bases. That's a valuable sign of a nascent rally. Then as the rally ages, fewer and fewer high-RS stocks will be in sound bases. They will become further and further extended. The leaders continue to extend, without new leaders coming up from behind out of sound bases. This tells me that a rally is looking a tad long in the tooth. I might choose to sell a few stocks to nail down a profit. I might get off margin if I have been on margin.

Or I might notice that a lot of high-RS stocks are starting to reverse *en masse* after staging attempted breakouts from bases. These are extremely useful signals, especially given the fact that since high-RS stocks lead the market, the behavior of these individual issues can alert you to trend changes ahead of the major averages. You get that handle on the market only by going through charts on a daily basis.

Q: *Can you elaborate on any theories and views concerning base building in a stock and how it provides a shelf from which a stock can move upward? What exactly is the "construction" that occurs in a basing period? Please discuss changes in stock ownership, overhead supply, and how prior resistance points lose strength after a constructive base-building period.*

Answered by Loren Fleckenstein 2000-04-22

Good question. I think chart patterns make much more sense if you understand the kind of behavior of the buyers and sellers who shaped the pattern.

Let's take a straightforward correction-recovery pattern, like a cup or a cup-and-handle. The idea behind such patterns is that you want to climb aboard a strong, advancing stock, but you don't want to get shaken out in a normal pullback due to profit-taking. Big winners undergo many such pullbacks.

So imagine that you have your eye on an attractive stock. Its company has strong earnings growth. It has high relative strength. It is in a long uptrend. The industry group is strong.

You wait for the stock to correct. This gets you out of the way of the profit-takers.

Now the stock faces a different problem. There are investors or traders who bought the stock just before the correction. So they have paper losses. We call these shareholders "weak holders" or "weak hands" because they have a tendency to sell into subsequent rallies to end their unpleasant experience in the stock. Their selling can dampen a stock's recovery. The amount of stock in these weak hands is called "overhead supply."

So just as you waited for a correction, now you wait for a recovery. You want to see the stock make up at least half of the point-loss from the last intraday high and the intraday low of the correction. You also want the stock above its 50- and 200-day moving averages. By doing this, the stock is showing that it has chewed through most of that overhead supply.

It's fine if you see some volume spikes along the bottom, especially if the stock ends the day on the high of the day's trading range. This shows people bailing out, and then new investors rushing in. So weak holders are replaced with new, hopefully stronger holders. This is "constructive" behavior, in that weaknesses in the stock are being replaced with strengths.

Another "constructive" sign is a price recovery on strong volume with pullbacks on light volume. This indicates more buying than selling in the stock. More of the stock is in strong hands than weak hands.

Finally, as the stock nears its pre-correction high, you may see it drift sideways or downward. Often people who bought near the bottom regard the old high as their selling point to take profits. Plus, you may have a final batch of weak holders head for the exits at this price level. It's "constructive" if this drift is downward (as defined by the lows of daily price bars) and on light volume.

That indicates that the last of the sellers are getting out of the way, but the selling is not so overwhelming as to raise doubts about the stock's ability to sustain further advances. Selling is muted. Most shareholders are content to hold onto their shares at the current market price. This will oblige new buyers in the future to bid up the price if heavy demand for the stock occurs.

Trading Breakouts

Q: *I follow Loren Fleckenstein's commentaries very carefully. Could you please explain a stock like EMLX or IDPH? If I missed purchasing around the breakout point (EMLX 130 and IDPH 175, approx.), how can I get in with the stocks being so extended from their bases? They move so quickly that by the time I see them in the evening, they are already 15.00 above their breakout points.*

Answered by Loren Fleckenstein 2000-10-28
From your question, I take it that you are looking at your target stocks once a day, maybe even after the close. I know of only one way to consistently catch breakouts in time to buy before the target stock becomes extended and vulner-

able to a pullback. You must monitor the market intraday. If you cannot have your eye glued to a computer screen during trading hours, at least consider some kind of real-time alert that will notify you once a stock has exceeded your pivot so you can take action. Of course, immediately set a price stop where you will sell to protect yourself against a severe loss in case the market turns against you. Also, limit your risk by position sizing.

Q: *Once a stock breaks out from a sound base, is it imperative that this breakout be confirmed (by volume) on the following day? If yes, must the volume again be at least 40%–50% higher than the average on the confirmation day?*

Answered by Kevin Marder 2000-09-09
On the breakout day, I like to see volume be at least 50% greater than its 50-day average. Though certainly preferable, I don't insist on volume being a certain amount on the day after the breakout day.

Q: *The current market environment has an air of uncertainty as to future direction and follow-through. Stocks that report earnings that disappoint or hint of future disappointment in this kind of market environment are often severely punished. Given that a stock meets CANSLIM criteria and is breaking out a few days before the earnings announcement, would you take a position at the pivot point? If not, I would appreciate a brief discussion of how you approach new positions during the earnings-reporting season.*

Answered by Greg Kuhn 2000-07-15
Very simply, I just buy 'em. The market knows many things ahead of time. A stock breaking out to new highs just before an earnings report may be telling you something good about the report. Just remember: There's always something to worry about. We're always dealing with incomplete information. You have to learn to trust what the market is telling you. In the case of three companies that warned about their earnings (BMCS, ENTU and CA), two of them (BMCS and CA) were already in deep downtrends, and the third (ENTU) was attempting to turn higher from a very deep correction (a 73%

drop) and was still about 50% from its old high. So something was already wrong with each of them.

Q: *With many stocks being so volatile, a stock will often increased more than 5% above the ideal "pivot point" for purchase within the FIRST day of the breakout. How do you then purchase this stock, as the strategy says not to chase them? Also, you can't really confirm a 40% increase in volume until AFTER the first day of the breakout. It seems "you're out" before you can even get in.*

Answered by Kevin Marder 2000-07-01
The objective is to buy a stock immediately after it breaks out of a base, be it a cup-and-handle base, flat base, etc. This means you buy a stock DURING a trading session, before it moves up more than 5% past its pivot point. At the time of breakout, you must note the volume thus far that day and extrapolate what you believe it will be by day's end. For example, if a stock breaks out at 12:15 P.M. ET, I double the current volume to give me the expected volume by day's end. Thanks very much for your question.

Q: *A lot of times I find out about the breakout after the market has closed, but the stock has moved $20 from the breakout point. Where should I be buying after a breakout?*

Answered by Mark Boucher 2000-10-07
The place to buy after a breakout is 1/8 of a point above the highest price of the price consolidation area that your stock is breaking out of, or at least very near to the breakout. Here is a way to avoid the situation you've described. When you find a potential breakout formation: Enter a buy stop at the aforementioned price. For the stocks that it sounds like you trade (i.e., stocks that move 20 points in a day), it's best to limit your risk by SIZING your order to the stock's volatility, so make your buy stop order for a smaller number of shares—no more than 100 shares, tops.

Q: *I have a question on pivot points at the time I'm watching for a stock to breakout. I'll use the example of NVDA for today. By the time the volume comes in at 150% ADV for the breakout, the pivot point is long gone. I've been watching*

NVDA for a while. I bought in today when the volume actually reached 1.3 million. At that point, the price was $146, past the pivot. There is absolutely no way you can buy within 1/8 of a point of a breakout. At that point, there is no volume to tell you that the stock is breaking out. Today, NVDA opened strong. Within the first hour, it was up to 135, but the volume of 300,000 did not strike me as great shakes. So I went about my business, only to return to see a definite breakout on strong volume. Too many times I have missed a breakout by a few hours, chose to pass on the stock, and then wanted to shoot myself a couple of days or weeks later. SDLI and ELNT are recent examples. So, back to my question: What, if any, road signs could help me? Or am I OK to wait for the volume, even though the price may be extended at that point?

Answered by Greg Kuhn 2000-06-24

The best way to tackle this is twofold. First, you can just buy the stock after it crosses 1/8 above its pivot point and before volume confirms, and then hope volume confirms by the end of the day. If volume doesn't confirm by the end of the day, but if the stock closes above its pivot price, you can wait an additional day. (On rare occasions, volume won't immediately confirm by being 40% higher than average, but it will confirm on the second day.) If volume doesn't confirm by the second day, sell the position outright.

Also, you can extrapolate a day's trend in volume as a stock is breaking out to see if the volume would be sufficient to confirm. For example, if a stock needs to trade 400,000 on a potential breakout day to be 40% higher than average (for a valid breakout), and if at noon, as the stock seems to be breaking out, the volume already is 250,000, then the stock can be bought right there. (Divide 250,000 by 2.5—2.5 hours into trading session—and multiply that figure by 6.5—the number of hours in a session. In this example, the 250,000 volume at noon extrapolates to 650,000 shares at the close).

Q: Do you wait for a pullback or consolidation to buy? Should we see a pullback to a breakout area?

Answered by Loren Fleckenstein 2000-06-17

I think your actual options relate to buying on breakouts or buying on pullbacks. It's not an either/or proposition. You can buy on breakouts as a stock advances through its pivot point, and you can buy the same stock as it pulls back, assuming it does not drop back into the prior base. If you also use volume cues, trading volume should expand on breakouts and contract on pullbacks. Now, that said, in my experience as an intermediate-term trader, I find proper breakouts have a higher probability of success than pullbacks. Other traders may have a different experience. For instance, one trader may just be better at spotting a sound pullback than a sound breakout. But generally speaking, I like to enter a new position in the same direction as the trade. Buying on a pullback, the stock is moving in the opposite direction of where you want it to be going. To me, that implies added risk. But again, this is not to rule out pullbacks as a valid entry tactic.

Q: *I recently spotted a stock that had formed a sound flat base after a strong prior uptrend. The market opened and the stock then proceeded to go through the pivot point. I determined that the volume was more than 50% higher than the 50-day average volume by breaking the 50-day average volume down into hourly increments. This revealed that the volume was approximately 50% higher than normal for the first hour of trading. The price moved up throughout the day, but I then saw a disturbing problem . . . the total volume for the breakout day was only going to end up being average, at best. I guess the buyers just didn't continue stepping up to the plate in large numbers like I would have preferred. The stock came back a little bit, but still closed up for the day. If this was your trade, would you: 1. Hang onto the stock, even though the final volume was going to be mediocre? 2. Sell it for a small profit and move on, or repurchase if the volume firmed up? I sold it. It will probably rocket at the open tomorrow!*

Answered by Kevin Marder 2000-04-01

The mechanics of your trade appear sound. Having most of the volume appear in the early stages of a session is something that often occurs and can't be avoided if you buy early in the day. Instead of comparing the day's volume in a stock with that of its 50-day moving average of volume, I often compare the day's volume with that of the prior day. As far as whether to sell before the end of the entry day, if volume looks as though it won't be particularly heavy versus its 50-day moving average of volume, this should be looked at on a case-by-case situation. Unless the stock really acts poorly later during the entry day, I find myself usually holding on until the next day to see if there's any follow-through on stepped-up volume. An obvious thing to check out is how the stock closes, i.e., is it in the top quartile of its entry-day range? Also, what is the general market doing that day? If the general market is weakening in the afternoon, yet the stock holds in pretty well, perhaps it's the weight of the overall market that's keeping a lid on the stock's volume. I'm sorry there's no easy answer to this, but it's just another nuance of trading that is probably best solved via your own experience.

Q: *It is my understanding that the stocks that break out before or on a follow-through day are usually the leaders during the next advance. Are you often faced with the dilemma of seeing the first stocks to breakout being more than 5% beyond the exact pivot point when the follow-through day arrives? If so, do you purchase? How do you handle this?*

Answered by Greg Kuhn 2000-04-22
In my experience, very few will break out prior to a follow-through day. However, I've witnessed several strong leaders actually break out on the follow-through day. If any one stock is extended by more than 5% above its breakout point, I pass, but keep my eye on it nonetheless. In some cases, usually depending on what the market does just after its follow-through-day signal, one of the stocks I missed may immediately go into a four- or five-week base 10%–20% above its original breakout. This is where I've typically found "flat" bases form—after a breakout from a larger base. If one of these bases form, then I'll try to catch the next breakout. Please bear in mind, though, that a strong bull run—one that's worth being involved in on the long side—will be carried by many stocks with leading characteristics. In fact, according to Bill O'Neil's historical studies and something that I've seen first-hand, leading stocks will continuously breakout for up to 13 weeks following a follow-through day that kicks off a new bull market. If I miss one, like the Long Island Railroad, another train is right behind.

Anticipating

Q: *How can I avoid missing breakouts that have exceeded my low-risk buy point by the time I see them? Should I consider early entry prior to the breakout, or if I've missed the breakout, hope I get a pullback, or maybe establish a buy stop just above the breakout?*

Answered by Kevin N. Marder 2000-03-25

By lowering your purchase price below the pivot point, you are taking on more risk. The risk is that some investors that bought near the old high will try to sell and break even. If you buy the stock too early, you will have to fight your way through overhead resistance. Buying at the right time is critical for your trading success. If you cannot follow the market intraday, look into some of the services that alert you when a stock hits a specific price/volume specification. If you miss the initial breakout, wait for a safe entry point, as many stocks offer new entry opportunities a few days or weeks later.

Finally, be sure not to buy a stock that has risen 5% or more from the pivot point. Also, set a stop-loss price on every new purchase that will cause you to sell and cut your losses if the stock breakout fails and turns against you. Many intermediate-term traders sell any new buy that falls 8% below their purchase price. As the stock advances, you can use a trailing stop, which will cause you to take profits if the stock reverses, rather than waiting for the stock to give up all your gains before selling.

Q: *I am new to trading and inexperienced at recognizing breakouts. Subscribing to your site has been very helpful. I bought ORCL Thursday at 64 1/2, thinking it would break out, but then it dipped after hitting a new high. Then Friday, it took off on much heavier volume. What chart pattern would you say ORCL fits at this time? I'm concerned that it has not been in this base for very long after splitting. Does that make it a less-than-excellent candidate for the long term?*

Answered by Eddie Kwong 2000-03-04

Breakouts are among the trickiest forms of setups to trade. The best way to answer your question about Oracle is to help you to understand what kinds of ingredients we need to see in any breakout. Then you can not only draw your own conclusion about Oracle, but also have the tools necessary to have better results trading breakouts in general. You have to look at a wide range of factors in order to turn the odds as much in your favor as possible. Whether you're watching a stock break out to new all-time highs from consolidation, or from some classical chart pattern, you must never buy into a breakout until you consider the following factors:

- **The stock should be part of a hot group.** This way it will not only be carried by its own momentum, but by the momentum of the group it belongs to.

- **The stock should be near an all-time high.** You don't want to be buying a stock that is "bottoming out" because in order to go up, such a stock often has to fight through overhead resistance. That is, the frustrated owners of the stock who had previously bought in at higher levels will look for opportunities to get out at their break-even levels. A stock thus affected could easily fizzle out after the breakout.

- **Ideally, look for breakouts to all-time highs that occur from long narrow trading ranges of three months or more**. The long quiet, once interrupted, often leads to explosive, sustained moves.

- **When trading breakouts from short pullbacks, look for tight, narrow-range pullbacks.** Breakouts from these tend to be cleaner, and it's easier to tell at the outset whether or not the breakout will fail or succeed.

- **Make sure there's sturdy support not far below your entry point.** This sturdy support will usually come from the lows of the trading range or a pullback from which a stock is breaking out.

- **Regardless of what type of breakout you trade, always look for volume support.** Ideally, the breakout day should be accompanied by a large volume spike and the stock should close near its high of the day. Not only should the stock continue higher, but also when it runs into the inevitable pullback, that pullback should be on light volume, so that you know traders are holding onto the stock.

There are other rules governing the use of breakouts in your trading. For further information, I highly recommend that you check out Greg Kuhn and Kevin Marder's Intermediate-Term Momentum Trading Course and Week 2 and Week 3 of Mark Boucher's Short-Term Trading Course.

Q: *How do I determine volume on a stock ready to breakout after the market has been open for 30 minutes? I can look at a chart in retrospect and with hindsight say, yep, there's that damn buy point. But in the heat of the battle, I find confusion reigns. "Is that higher-than-normal volume?," I ask myself, and "Is the rise in price just some intraday volatility?" I do not find that I have a handle on the buy point and volume considerations in the early hours of the market. And if you do make a purchase and within the hour the stock drops 8% and you get stopped out, when do you consider getting in again? How do you know the stock hasn't just entered into a trading range of 15% for a few days, and you could be getting in and stopped out a number of times?*

Answered by Sterling Ten 2000-04-08

Generally, a trader will view a price breakout accompanying 1.5 times the 50-day average volume as a buy signal on the stock. Traders will usually buy the stock at the end of the day if it meets the criteria. However, you can also cheat and buy the stock during the day. To do this, the stock must be breaking out of the base with at least 1/2 of the 1.5 times average volume by 12:15 P.M. ET, the midpoint of a trading day. Normally, the midpoint should be at 12:45 P.M., but since the volume during the first half-hour of trading is usually heavier, we adjust the midpoint in this case to be 12:15 P.M. If you get stopped out, you can re-enter the stock if it breaks out again, as long as the stock is not materially extended above its most recent base. By "materially extended," I mean the stock is trading 5%–10% above the top of the base.

Base on Top of a Base

Q: *For Greg Kuhn: During this latest meltdown, I see some stocks that didn't make big corrections. In fact, some stocks, such as PWER and PCCC, just kept flying. Their charts show that they just keep piling on base after base.*

When do we know to make exceptions about buying off of a third- or fourth-stage base in stocks like this? I have heard that bases become "reset" if a correction forces their price below the low of the previous base. If this never happens, do we just assume that because the general indexes corrected that their bases are now "reset" also?

Answered by Greg Kuhn 2000-07-08

The base "count" begins only after at least a five-week base, after a prior reaction low is breached to reset the base count. The small bases that PWER and PCCC developed during their recent runs would not count as multiple bases. PCCC broke out from Base #1 on April 18, while PWER broke out from a base-on-base pattern, Base #1 on March 7, and from Base #2 on May 12. Both stocks did emerge as leaders while the Nasdaq struggled into Q2, but there's

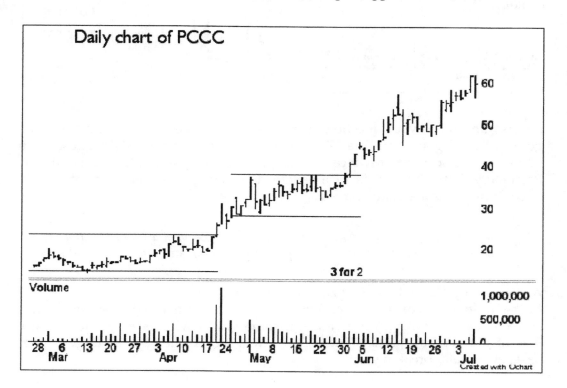

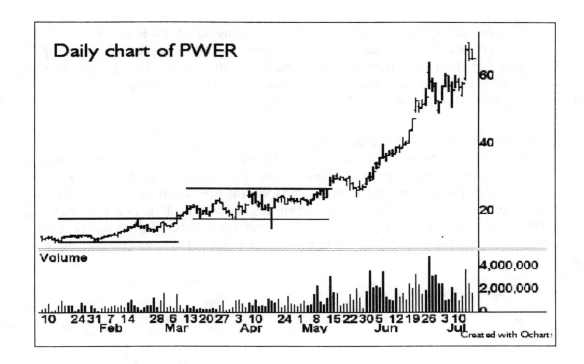

Daily chart of PWER

no easy answer to your question. Just remember: Three out of four stocks will go down during a serious market decline. But this fact obviously suggests that one in four stocks can advance. It's just a matter of playing the probabilities. Personally, if the market is in a severe downswing, I don't want to be involved; the odds are against me.

Q: *Mr. Marder, please clarify the concept of a base-on-top-of-a-base formation. I have studied your excellent trading course, but I am still unclear on the concept.*

Answered by Kevin Marder 2000-05-27
In the middle or near the end of either an 8% to 12% intermediate-term market correction or an outright bear market, some stocks will resist the downward bias of the general market. These issues will move sideways as they form a base, eventually breaking out.

But due to the bearish trend of the general market, these stocks will exhibit little follow-through on their breakouts. Instead, they will build another base just above the prior base that they had broken out of. Often, when a fresh intermediate advance is kicked off in the general market, these stocks will prove themselves among the new leaders.

One example of this base-on-top-of-a-base phenomenon is Oracle. The stock built a base from July 19, 1999, to Sept. 3, 1999, before breaking out. It then built another base from Sept. 10 to Oct. 29, before breaking out on Nov. 1. From there, it spurted about 160% over the next two months—quite a feat for such a large-cap stock.

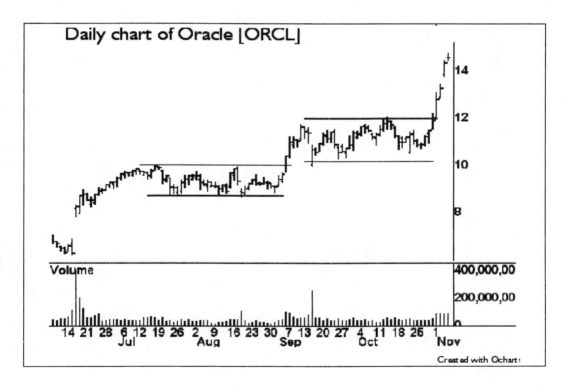

See also, CUP-AND-HANDLES, page 131.

CHAPTER 4

Harnessing the Power of Momentum

You've heard that the "trend is your friend." The term "momentum" in its use in modern trading is a way of describing the strength of a trend.

With the press that "momentum trading" has gotten recently, you'd think that it is some kind of new invention. In reality, momentum and the use of it by traders is not a new force that has suddenly started tossing the market around in the late 1990s—rather, it is a mode of price movement that has been around since the beginning of the financial markets. In fact, the patterns that momentum traders use to hop on board strong, powerful trends are not drastically different from those that are clearly visible in charts of the earliest recorded price and volume action in the markets.

OK . . . so the patterns have always been there. But there is something that occurred during the late 1990s that does set the present era apart from the past.

The difference is in the popularization of practical techniques for capturing fast directional moves in the market. One man many credit with developing a systematic and scientific framework for traders to use in capturing fast directional moves in the markets is *Jeff Cooper. A professional daytrader long before anyone knew what that was, Cooper described the exact recipes for his success in exploiting momentum in his now classic book* Hit and Run Trading: The Short-Term Stock Trader's Bible. *Whether Cooper's work was a major catalyst or simply arrived on the scene at good time, the release of Cooper's book in the mid-1990s coincided with the birth of a legion of highly successful momentum traders—and their number is growing every day. A big industry consisting of online brokerages, computerized trading and analysis platforms, and trading houses was also spawned.*

There are many methodologies from a variety of brilliant traders that are discussed in this chapter besides Jeff Cooper. I don't mean to imply that any of them took the lead from Jeff. But in my mind, Jeff can be credited with drawing attention to momentum and its potential as a powerful tool for traders to hop on board the fast-moving freight trains that markets often become.

PULLBACKS FROM HIGHS

Q: For Dave Landry: In your "Stock and Futures Outlook" columns, you often point out charts pulling back two to three bars in a strong uptrending market (and vice versa for bear markets). Could you comment on how much emphasis you give these setups in your own trading and tell me a bit more on how you trade them? That is, enter at yesterday's high, open + % of range, etc.?

Answered by Dave Landry 2000-05-20
It's amazing that in this day and age, with all of the technology available, that something as simple as a two-to-three-bar pullback in a strong trend still works. Yes, I consider these setups valid. In fact, in trading, the simpler the concept, the better.

I normally like to see at least three days in a pullback, but I will consider a two-bar pullback, especially if it comes off of a reversal-type day. In other words, the stock or future hits a new high and reverses on the same day.

As far as entry, I always like to see some sort of follow-through in the direction of the intended trade. Therefore, if looking to go long, I might look to enter when it takes out the prior day's high. The methods you described above also make sense to me, as they are with the trend.

The low of the formation (a) provides a logical point to place your initial protective stop. The first profit target would be the old highs (b). At this point, you might want to take off a piece and move your stops to break-even on the remainder. Read my articles on pullbacks and money management under Trader's Lessons for more info here.

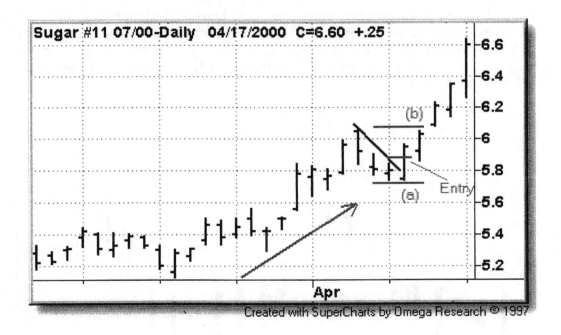

One last point: Keep in mind that two- to three-bar pullbacks are not rocket science or some sort of magical setup. Most people easily recognize the pattern(s). Therefore, there always exists the chance of false moves out of these setups. However, by nature of the pullback, it normally gives a good profit-to-risk ratio when it does work.

Q: *Jeff Cooper, I read an article of yours that mentioned a "V-thrust buy signal" after a three-day pullback. Could you please explain what that is and when you can use that setup as a buy signal? By the way, I found your* 5 Day Momentum *book extremely useful and easy to understand.*

Answered by Jeff Cooper 2000-10-07

The V-Thrust is a pattern in which a strongly uptrending stock experiences a sharp selloff and then thrusts higher. The rules for the setup are: (1) The stock must have made a 60-day high within the past seven trading sessions; (2) A sharp three- to six-day selloff must ensue; (3) During the prior day, the stock must have risen above the previous day's high, forming the beginning of the "V" formation; and (4) The next day only, buy 1/16 above the prior day's high. I give several examples of this pattern and how to trade it in my book *Hit and Run Trading II.*

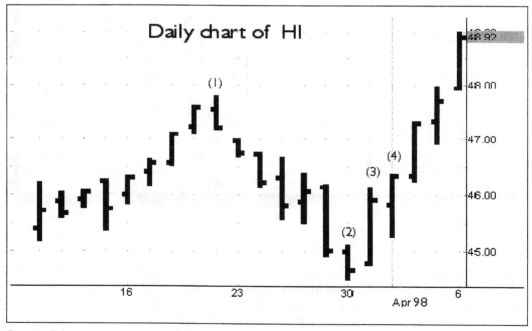

Source: Qcharts.

CHAPTER 4

Q: *I have been getting some experience trying pullback strategies and would appreciate you sharing your experience in order to accurately form my own expectations. How often, percentage-wise, do pullback purchases of a trending stock: a) reverse after correct entry, resulting in a multi-point loss; b) advance a small amount, and then reverse, typically resulting in a scratched trade; c) advance just to the point of paying for losses in a); and, finally, d) advance an amount that really means something?*

Answered by Dave Landry 2000-09-30
First and foremost, pullbacks are a discretionary pattern. Everyone defines them differently. Even for a "defined" pullback like a Connors/Cooper 1-2-3-4 or my Trend Pivot Pullbacks, you wouldn't take every setup. You have to learn how to pick and choose the best. I consider the overall market conditions, the sector action, the volatility of the stock, the strength of the stock's trend, the volume (too thin? too thick?), the spread, how it closed, where I should enter (if taken) and so on and so forth. And if I take the trade, money management and position become crucial. Initial stop placement, trailing stops and profit-taking will vary from stock to stock.

If you do decide you want to "mechanize" pullbacks, I suggest you first quantify all of the above. For instance, first quantify the setup itself (i.e., a 1-2-3-4? a Trend Pivot Pullback?) and then quantify your rules: How do I define trend? Where should initial stops be placed? Dollar-based? Volatility-based? Pattern-based? Where should partial profits be taken? How should I trail stops? You'll also have to specifically quantify things you've asked such as "really means something?"

Q: *I like to buy on dips. What is the key criterion to ascertain whether a stock is pulling back versus a stock that is going into a longer-term downtrend?*

Answered by Dave Landry 1999-09-25
By buying on dips, I assume you mean Pullbacks From Highs. The idea behind buying pullbacks is like catching a ride on a freight train. You can't catch it when it's really moving, but if it slows a bit, you might be able to hop on

and ride the momentum. However, if you wait until it completely stops, then you don't get anywhere (or you possibly go in the wrong direction). The trick is knowing when it is just slowing and not stopping (or in the process of changing direction). In stocks, I like to see a 5% to 10% pullback from highs. For instance, if a stock hits a new high at 100, the stock may offer a buying opportunity as it pulls back to 90 to 95, provided it shows some signs that its uptrend has resumed (e.g., it begins to rally and takes out the prior two- to three-bar high).

However, if the stock continues to sell off and drops 15% or more from highs, you have to begin to question whether the original uptrend remains intact or if a downtrend has begun.

Created with SuperCharts by Omega Research © 1996

Let's look at Policy Management Systems (PMS), a stock that recently pulled back, but subsequently failed. Notice at point (a) that the stock is in a strong uptrend. Then at (b) it pulls back from highs. This suggests the stock may be consolidating before heading higher. But the stock continues to drift/sell off, and by point (c) you have to begin to wonder if the original uptrend is still intact. Also, notice that at no time after (b) did the stock have a significant rally (take out the prior two- to three-bar highs).

One last point, the more volatile the stock, the more it can pullback and then resume its uptrend. For instance, a high-flying technology stock may correct 20% (or more) and then resume its uptrend.

Q: *I track stocks that appear on the 60-day New High list, and I continue to follow them when they pull back. When they correct or consolidate, how long do you watch them? Is there some pullback level at which they drop out of consideration?*

Answered by Dave Landry 1999-10-07

You are correct in watching stocks from the New 60-Day Highs on Double Volume List for pullbacks. Often these stocks pull back and then resume their uptrends.

In general, you have to look at two things when judging pullbacks:

1. The depth of the selloff, and the time that has elapsed.

2. If the stock drops too much, you have to wonder if the initial trend is still intact. In other words, a pullback should be viewed as a pause in trend. Once it becomes more than a pause, then a new downtrend possibly has begun.

In general, I like to see stocks pull back about 5% to 10% from new highs. I've seen more volatile issues (i.e., IPOs, high-flying technology stocks, and so on) pull back 20% (or more) and subsequently rally to new highs.

As far as time, the longer the stock goes without rallying, the more you should question the original trend. In other words, is the lackluster action a sign the original momentum has dried up? With that said, I normally like to see a stock pull back for no more than 12 days since the new high. If the stock is in an incredibly strong uptrend, I may extend that figure a few days. By the same token, you may want to be less lenient for stocks in weaker uptrends.

Q: *A lot of the pullback stocks you highlight in your nightly Outlook commentary, although in good intermediate-term up-moves, often look very much like they are forming classic Edwards/Magee descending-triangle formations (i.e., progressively weaker attempts to rally from new support). How do you distinguish between bearish triangle patterns that perhaps should be avoided and juicy pullback opportunities? Is it just that the since the dominant trend is up, the classification of the short-term pattern as bearish is less relevant as a predictor?*

Answered by Dave Landry 2000-03-25
Great question! The "classical" right triangle pattern is a bigger-picture pattern. The theory is that the sellers (a) meet and break through support (b).

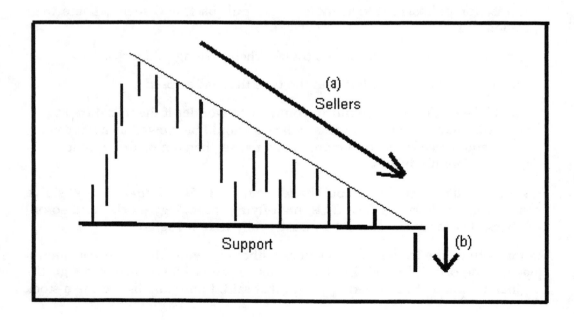

Often the pullbacks I consider have created "mini" right triangles. However, I view it as bullish as the underlying strong uptrend often prevails. Further, I see a breakout above the triangle as an entry and the bottom of the triangle (support) as a great place to put my protective stop (b).

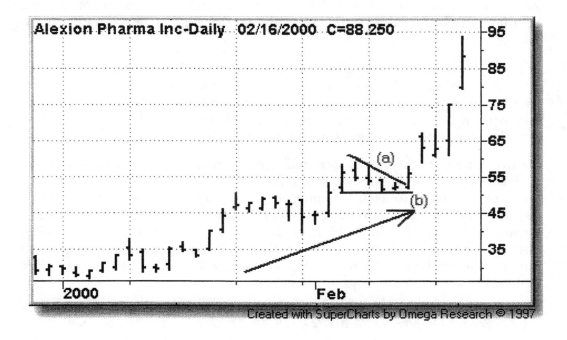

Q: *Jeff, I see that you have a few lists at the bottom of your commentary (Pull-backs, Complex Pullbacks, Continuation Setups, etc.). Could you explain these to me? I understand what a pullback is. I just want to know the implications of these things and what a complex pullback and continuation setup are. Are all the stocks that you have listed at the bottom of your commentary bullish? Also, do you use volume as an indicator when deciding which trade to make? If so, what volume clues do you look for when determining to go long (short)?*

Answered by Jeff Cooper 2000-04-01

To begin with, I do look at volume, but I've seen big moves on small volume and big moves on gigantic volume, so the price and pattern remain my primary consideration.

As for complex pullbacks, not always do you get a straight-line pullback, but you sometimes get zigzag or A-B-C patterns. Or you get a first pivot up, and then it comes back and tests the low of the pullback again before it goes up in earnest.

A continuation setup basically occurs at a point of equilibrium where an uptrending stock looks like it's sold out and it's sort of starting up again where I can see continuation. Typically, in my experience, short-term momentum lasts anywhere from one to three days. If there are real buyers, they don't just disappear into the wings after just their first day.

On the same note, sometimes you will see big momentum, and then they lay off for a day or two. You may still want to stalk it because they will come back for it, so you want to keep watching it. There may have been continuation a day or so before, and I'm looking for a continuation of that momentum. Again, regarding volume, if I'm looking to short a stock that really hasn't broken down yet, and it's still above its rising 10- and 50-day moving averages, I will look for distribution at the top on bigger volume than when it was going up, and I will look for down days where volume increases.

Q: *For Jeff Cooper: On Wednesday, July 19, I believe you mentioned a possible 1-2-3-4 buy setup in the S&Ps. You are one of my mentors, and I know a couple of your patterns inside and out. The 1-2-3-4 is one of my favorites from you and Larry Connors. When you mentioned the 1-2-3-4 setup in the S&Ps, I immediately asked if the ADX had risen high enough to make this work? I checked, and sure enough, the ADX for the S&Ps was around 11.00—signaling that the market is nearly at a standstill. Jeff, ADX above 35 is one of your rules for trading a 1-2-3-4. I know it well, because I really tried to break that rule, and the pattern failed every time. With the S&P showing an ADX of about 11.00 (which means the S&Ps are not trending strongly), what prompted the 1-2-3-4 buy setup in your commentary? Is there a new buy setup that you are using that I have missed?*

Answered by Duke Heberlein 2000-07-29

It is important to note *what* Jeff was saying in his commentary for the morning of July 19. He was referring to a *possible* 1-2-3-4 in the September S&P futures. Jeff wrote, "Whether the market is running into trouble here or Tuesday merely reflects normal profit-taking. It will probably take into next week to determine this. Earnings and options expirations will continue to spin prices into Friday, and even a typical 1-2-3-4 pullback will take us into Friday (July 21)." The 1-2-3-4 had not occurred; he was only speaking of what could happen in terms of overall market dynamics. It was not a specific buy setup.

MOMENTUM BREAKOUTS *(See also, BREAKOUTS, page 40)*

Bull Trap/Bear Trap

Q: *I can't find a description or chart example of a bull trap or a bear trap.*

Answered by Mark Etzkorn 1999-07-03

Bull and bear traps are essentially false breakout patterns. A bull trap occurs when an uptrending market breaks out to the upside of a congestion pattern (e.g., a trading range), but quickly reverses (usually within a few days) to the downside. A bear trap is simply the inverted form of this pattern that occurs at market bottoms.

When a previously uptrending market breaks out of congestion but fails to follow through, it is a sign there is little or no buying pressure to sustain a continued rally (in the case of a bull trap). Traders who bought into the "trap" soon scramble to get out of their positions, along with previous longs.

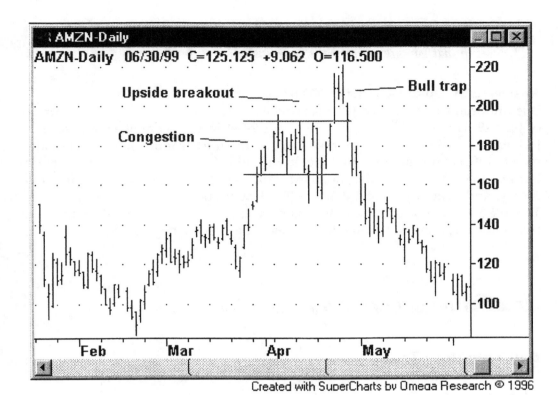

AMZN-Daily 06/30/99 C=125.125 +9.062 O=116.500

Upside breakout

Bull trap

Congestion

Feb   Mar   Apr   May

Created with SuperCharts by Omega Research © 1996

This chart shows a bull trap in Amazon.com (AMZN). A choppy congestion phase developed in late-March '99. An upside breakout occurred in April (the bull trap)—probably convincing many traders a new leg of the uptrend was underway—only to be reversed within three days. The subsequent down move was quite dramatic.

From Bases

Q: *My question pertains to a failed breakout that does not violate the purchase-loss cut point and how to handle that trade. A recent example would have been XLNX, which broke out on 10/29/99, and hit a new high on*

11/29/99, but by a week later was showing signs of distribution and turned back to touch the lip of the breakout. The O'Neil theory has it that a stock that makes a 20% or more move immediately after the breakout should be held for the duration of eight weeks. I understand that you do not comment on individual stocks, but I believe as much is to be learned from failure as success and your comments on this issue or others similar to this example would greatly help my trading abilities.

Answered by Kevin Marder 2000-04-29

I don't pay attention to the 20% rule that O'Neil speaks of. I instead wait for a stock to break down before I consider selling. Thus, in the XLNX example, I would have paid attention to how the stock was actually acting, as opposed to some sort of mechanical rule. Beginning with Dec. 1, you had six distribution days over an eight-day span, including four D-days in a row. This was excessive (!) and was the only information that you needed to know to sell.

Q: When a stock emerges out of a solid base on great volume, but dives back to the middle or bottom of that base in the next day or two, how does one determine the next entry point?

Answered by Dave Landry 2000-04-22

You are correct, in that you should consider exiting or be stopped out when trying to play a breakout of stock that dives back into its base. As far as re-entry, it depends on the pattern. If it doesn't go too deep into the base, then you could possibly play the breakout as it is rallying back towards old highs/top of the base. However, if it goes deep into the base or ever "undercuts" it, you might want to wait for a breakout above the entire base. As far as the "basing process," if it doesn't dive too far beneath the base, then the existing base remains intact.

From Flags

Q: Mark Boucher was explaining entering a trade out of a flag when he said something about when it is "TBBLBG," but then didn't explain what that stands for. My friends and I would really appreciate an explanation.

Answered by Marc Dupée 1999-06-19

Mark said: "My favorite pattern is a flag-pattern. Where a stock makes a strong run-up, consolidates and does not retrace 30% of the last advance, and then breaks out on a TBBLBG. You can use only that pattern and make a ton of money in the markets. It forces you to only buy strength."

TBBLBG stands for Thrust Breakout, Breakout Lag or Breakout Gap. The acronym describes one of three simple patterns that are present in 85% of all runaway markets. Any one of the three, TG, BL or BG, being present is sufficient to identify a runaway market. The acronym Mark has coined serves him as a mnemonic device to make sure that at least one of the three is present, and is not meant to be exclusionary or highfalutin.

I will leave you with an example in the sugar futures market depicting Breakout Laps and Breakout Gaps.

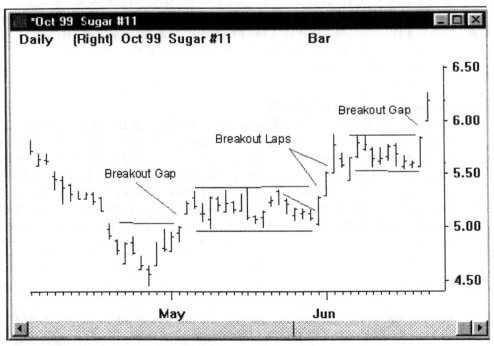

Source: RealTick by Townsend Analytics, Ltd.

Donchian Channel

Q: *What exactly are Donchian channels and how can they be used? Are they anything similar to linear regression channels?*

Answered by Mark Etzkorn 1999-09-11

It's not an indicator, *per se*. The term Donchian "channel" simply refers to the breakout trading approach first popularized by Richard Donchian in the 1960s and 1970s. Donchian's basic breakout system was also called the "four-week rule": buy when price exceeds the highest high of the past four weeks and sell when price falls below the lowest low of the past four weeks—i.e., a 20-day breakout system.

This approach succeeds in getting you in trending moves whenever they occur (you're buying when a market is showing strength and selling when it's showing weakness), at the cost of extensive drawdowns because of excessive whipsaw trades (repeated false breakout signals) in non-trending market periods. In practice, longer "channels," or time periods (e.g., 40 days or more), are generally used as the basis for trend trading systems.

This staple of the trend-followers' trading arsenal was further popularized in the late 1970s by the Turtles, Richard Dennis' now famous/infamous group of breakout disciples.

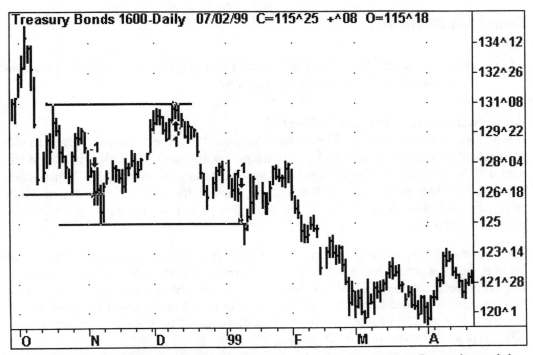

A 20-day Donchian-channel breakout system yields three trades in this downtrending market period.
Source: SuperCharts by Omega Research.

The chart above shows the signal from a 20-day (four-week) Donchian channel breakout system in the T-bond futures. The up and down arrows mark long and short entries, respectively, and the horizontal lines mark the 20-day highs and lows that were penetrated.

When is a "Breakout" a "Breakout"?

Q: *When I read about a particular support or resistance price, does it mean that if the stock moves past it by a tick, the level has been "officially" violated and a trade signal is given? Or is there a larger, minimum-amount move we should look for before acting on such breakouts?*

Answered by Mark Etzkorn 1999-11-06

Support and resistance levels are rarely precise price levels. When they appear to be, you should consider it more of a coincidence than as evidence that the market is being drawn to some "magic number."

For the most part, markets advance and retreat to general price levels, not exact prices. The more obvious a prior support or resistance level is, the more likely the market will trade very close to it in the future, for the simple reason that many traders are very aware of it, and markets are, as we all know, manifestations of crowd psychology.

What you should look for is a sustained move through a support or resistance level, a move of a certain magnitude through such levels, or both. The object is to separate meaningless price fluctuations—market "noise"—from significant price moves.

For example, an intraday penetration of a support level, even by a significant amount (say, 1 point for a stock trading at $25), is much less significant if the market closes strongly back above the support level. (The Dow, by the way, retreated dramatically intraday from resistance on 11/2/99.) Obviously, the price action over the next several days would be critical: If the stock continued to drop consistently lower, incrementally probing below the support level, it might be ready for a significant downside move. If it instead moved higher, the penetration would more likely be a successful "test" of the support level.

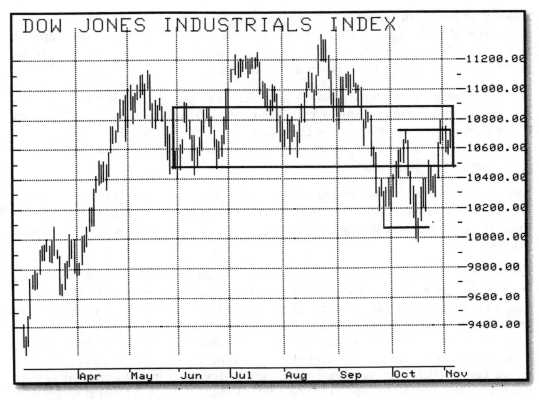

Source: Quote.com.

Here is a daily chart of the Dow Jones Industrial Average. The box marks a current resistance "zone" that has formed over the course of many months as the index established several relative lows and relative highs in the same general price vicinity. (Notice also how prior resistance becomes future support.) It is this level that the Dow is, as of 11/5/99, currently testing.

While the index has penetrated the relative high made in early October, it is too soon to say it has surpassed it for good. For evidence, just look at the mid-October penetration of the September relative low. The Dow dropped roughly 100 points below the most recent relative low, but it is obvious in retrospect that this support level was tested but not actually "broken."

CHAPTER 4

For the reasons we've outlined above, many breakout traders wait for confirming signals or look for additional follow-through when a support or resistance level is penetrated before taking any action. At the very least, you would want the market to close below a support level or above a resistance level to offer some proof that the breakout is meaningful. But a casual glance reveals what a weak requirement this is. It is more realistic to have to wait for several closes (say, for the sake of argument, five) before labeling a price move as a legitimate "violation" of a support or resistance level.

Another approach is to wait for the market to penetrate a price level by a certain percentage (e.g., 2%) to give evidence of exceptional price strength or weakness. To be useful, these kinds of approaches have to take into account the volatility of the market you're watching. More volatile markets require broader requirements.

Q: *David sometimes suggests letting a stock take out one- to two- or two- to three-bar highs (BEAS in his Outlook for Dec. 16). Does this mean breaking through a trendline, such as shown in the Dec. 17 Outlook, or does it mean going above the highs OF two or three days past?*

Answered by Dave Landry 1999-12-18

By "take out," I mean for the stock to trade intraday above its prior highs. This suggests that a stock is strong and may have resumed its uptrend. MRV Communications, a stock mentioned recently in the "Trading Outlook," provides a good example. Notice that the stock has been in a general uptrend. Also notice that during pullbacks/consolidations, the stock then re-asserts itself [at points (a), (b) and (c)], "taking out" (trading above) the prior highs and continuing higher.

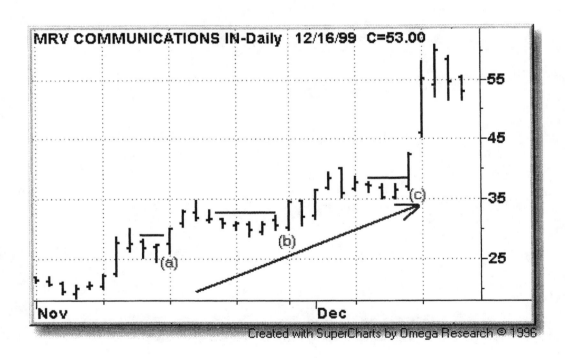

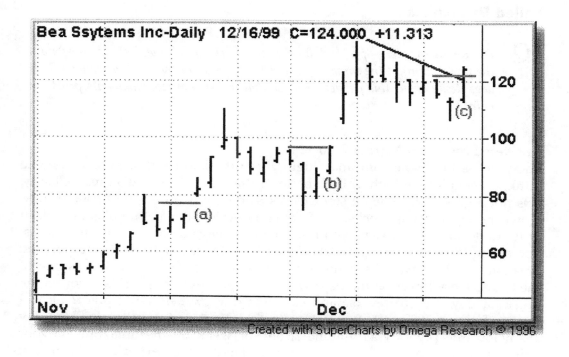

Bea Systems (BEAS), the stock you referred to above, also rallied nicely out of consolidations after taking out prior highs (a) and (b). At point (c), it has taken out both a trendline from highs and prior highs.

Failed Breakouts

Q: *For Kevin Marder—If a stock breaks out on heavy volume, but closes below the pivot point on the same day it breaks out, should the stock be sold? What does it say about this particular stock that it does not close above its pivot point?*

Answered by Kevin Marder 2000-12-09
The pivot is the highest intraday high within the handle, not, as some people think, a new all-time high. If both occur at the same time, that's great. Clearly, it is not a good sign when a stock closes below its pivot on the breakout day. However, big-winning stocks will frequently do just this before blasting off. In order to decide when to sell, you must look at things on a stock-by-stock basis. For example, was it the general market that caused it to pull back on the breakout day? Or was the general market strong, but your stock was one of the few to close lower on the day? Did the stock move 1% past its pivot on the breakout day, only to reverse and close the day 6% below the pivot? Or did the stock move 10% past its pivot on the breakout day, only to close the day 1% below the pivot? Was volume strong or weak on the breakout? If your stop-loss limit was 7%, was this level violated? With experience, you will know what to do, taking these and other variables into account.

Q: *If you enter a stock on a breakout and the stock then pulls back into its original base, is this an absolute sell, or is it just an indication to look for other criteria?*

Answered by Kevin Marder 2000-07-29
Many stocks will temporarily pull back into the top of their base following a breakout before driving ahead. I look at each situation differently and don't have a hard-and-fast rule here. If a stock moves up 10% and then pulls back into the base, I would be more tempted to sell it than if it moved up only 5% and then pulled back into the base. Use your analysis of the general market to guide you here. For example, if we're in a heady advance, and if other stocks

are breaking out and following through nicely, I'd be more apt to unload the stock and force-feed the money into another, more promising issue. By contrast, if the market is flat to weak, I'd give the stock a bit more slack. Additionally, sometimes I sell only half a position after it re-enters the base.

Q: *For Lewis Borsellino: You mention fake-outs. As a futures trader, my biggest cause of losses is being caught in failed breakouts, and my biggest cause of lost profits is not catching the real breakouts! What methods do you use to try to confirm that apparent breakouts are not actually fade-outs?*

Answered by Lewis Borsellino 2000-07-29
The two biggest determining factors are (a) time of day and (b) extensions. When it comes to time of day, we believe that the first 90 minutes of the trading day and the last 90 minutes of the trading day are the most valid when it comes to directional moves.

A close second in importance is extensions, vis-à-vis moving averages, in determining whether a move is a real move or is only a fake-out. For example, if we are 5% below the 20-day moving average, I would *not* expect us to see much more downward movement in this market, and thus, I would expect a fake-out.

Q: *I have a question concerning fast upside breakouts in general and the recent price action in Pacific Internet (PCNTF). This stock flew on Thursday (September 9, 1999) from 30 to 46, having had volatile moves on Tuesday and Wednesday. The stock then gapped up at 50 at the open on Friday and advanced to 54, just under its three-month or so high. After a pullback to 46 1/2, the stock advanced back to 51, flitted around 48–51 until about 12:00 P.M. Afternoon saw a steady decline to 40 on lower volume than Thursday. What are the indicators that the stock is under selling pressure before the actual decline has taken place? I would venture it was the inability to hold its initial gap up as one indicator (the pullback to 47, below its opening of 50) and the subsequent inability to advance meaningfully beyond its opening (a bounce off of 47 to 51). What is your take on it?*

Answered by Jeff Cooper 1999-09-18

Players who bought PCNTF on Thursday, Sept. 9 and stayed long overnight on the assumption Thursday's large-range day would attract buyers on Friday's (Sept. 10) open, gave those new buyers their stock based on the strong "gift horse" open.

Remember, despite the breakout over the 50-day moving average, the stock was still in a downtrend. One day does not a trend make; follow-through from a large impulse move and a series of higher lows is required. A move over the 50-day moving average or any resistance often is just the trick that triggers a short-covering capitulation or a buying binge, allowing someone with an agenda to sell into!

You've made a good observation. A stock that gaps open and then takes out the prior day's high to the downside, particularly a stock in a downtrend, is one indication to sell. Note that Friday was already the fourth large-range day. Spurts often occur over three to five days.

Now that PCNTF has pulled back a few days and tested its 50-day moving average, a low risk-to-reward long setup may be in the making (this answer was originally written on 9/15/99).

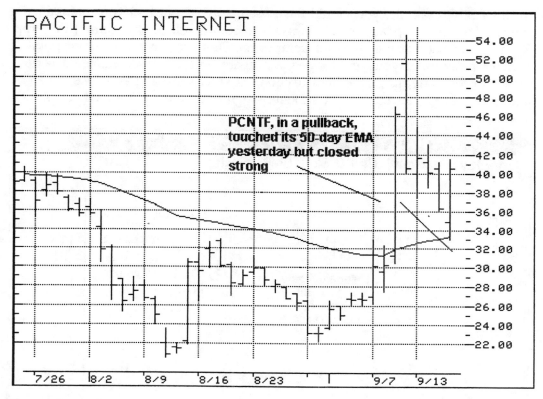

PACIFIC INTERNET

PCNTF, in a pullback, touched its 5D-day EMA yesterday but closed strong

Source: Quote.com.

Q: *Many traders discuss breakouts. Do they still take the trade if it hits the open protective stop (OPS) and turns and breaks out? Do you get back in?*

Answered by Marc Dupée 1999-06-11

If you've entered a trade and get jiggled out (your open protective stop, OPS, takes you out of your position), you can re-enter in the direction of your original trade at the breakout point if the setup still remains valid. You're probably going against your instincts to take a loss and enter a market in the same direction right after getting stung, but if conditions are right, it can be the correct choice.

In this CSCO example, you would have been stopped out had you maintained a tight, 1/4-point stop as Kevin Haggerty recommends in his Slim Jim setup. Re-enter the trade at the breakout point of the Slim Jim (or the breakout point of another pattern). If you get stopped out again and the price makes a serious breach of the pattern in the other direction, consider reversing your position: Violations of patterns are strong—or stronger—signals than the patterns themselves.

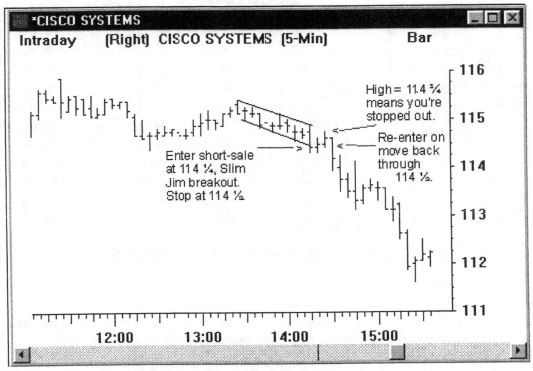

Re-entering CSCO after getting stopped out in the direction of the original breakout. Source Created with RealTick by Townsend Analytics, Ltd.

Q: *On 7/10/99, you spoke about an Amazon (AMZN) bull trap. (I was caught in that trap as I sold my AMZN puts shortly after the stock traded beyond its all-time high. I then watched in disgust as it quickly reversed and traded at about 120 at expiration.) I'm just wondering: Generally speaking, are false breakouts (e.g., bull and bear traps) as reliable to trade as "normal" breakouts? If I see a failed breakout, can I be more, less, or equally certain of the future direction as I am when trading a normal breakout pattern (e.g., cup-and-handle, flag, etc.)?*

Answered by Mark Etzkorn 1999-07-24

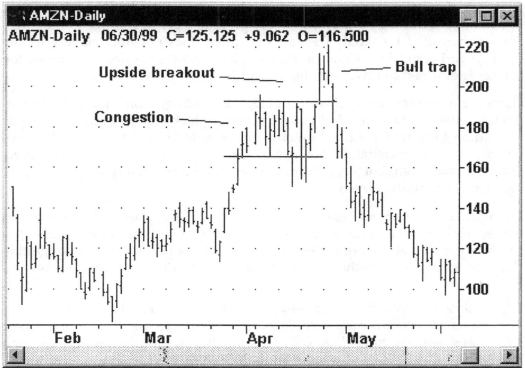

I don't know of a comprehensive study that has rigorously compared the success rates of breakouts to reversals following breakouts, but more than a few notable traders, including TradingMarkets' Jeff Cooper, argue that moves following failed signals are more reliable (and often more forceful) than regular breakout moves.

One of the reasons failed signals can provide such favorable trade opportunities is they are fueled by traders who entered on the original breakout move and are caught off-guard by the reversal. As a result, failed signals—especially those that occur after extended trends—often presage sharp turnarounds, as traders expecting a trend continuation realize the end has finally come.

A "false" trade signal, say, an upside trading-range breakout that drifts back down into the trading range, may simply precede a genuine move in the direction of the initial breakout. The fact that price does not immediately follow through and result in a significant trend (or continuation) does not mean the market is destined to reverse to the downside.

However, consider the following quote from *Schwager on Futures: Technical Analysis* (1996, John Wiley & Sons, New York) which was recently featured as a "Trading Insight of the Day" on our site: "A failed signal is among the most reliable of all chart signals. When a market fails to follow through in the direction of a chart signal, it very strongly suggests the possibility of a significant move in the opposite direction."

But ultimately, your success will be determined by your risk control and money management. One of the reasons traders use time delays and other confirmation signals before taking breakout trades is to limit the risk of getting chopped up in the noise that frequently occurs at obvious breakout levels.

Q: *Greg, I understand that you and many other market technicians feel that increased volume is a key factor in deciding when to go long, but could it also be said that increased volume is a contrary indicator? Also, do you have specific rules to determine when a real breakout is? Also, what about using volume to go short or at least knowing when to get out? After a protracted run-up (downturn), would an increase in volume be bullish (bearish)?*

Answered by Greg Kuhn 2000-03-25
Volume must be used prudently. Heavy upside volume in a base is bullish: no

ifs, ands or buts about it. However, heavy upside volume well into a stock's advance can actually be bearish. It all depends where the volume is coming in—in the base, or well past the base breakout.

As for sufficient volume on a breakout, 40% above the stock's 50-day moving average of volume is minimum. If a stock is breaking out during the day and volume is nowhere near the 40% mark, I will extrapolate the volume out to the end of the day at that point in determining whether or not it's sufficient.

Let's say a stock needs 400,000 shares to meet this minimum parameter on its breakout, but at 11:30 A.M. ET, only has 150,000. I'll divide the 150,000 by two (two hours into the trading day), and multiply that by 6 1/2 (6 1/2 hours in the trading day). In this example, the extrapolated volume is 487,500 shares (150,000/2 × 6 1/2), which is sufficient enough at that point to buy it.

If by the end of trading the stock closed above its breakout, but volume didn't confirm, I'll hold the stock for one more day. In rare occasions, volume will confirm on the second day. If it doesn't, I sell it outright.

Frankly, I usually don't even wait for the volume to confirm during the day. I just buy it and hope it confirms by the end of the day. If you wait for the volume extrapolation to confirm during the session, sometimes the stock is already well into its breakout—especially with some Internet stocks. However, again, if volume doesn't confirm that day, or the next, I sell it outright.

On the short side, volume is a lot trickier. Sometimes, the heavy volume downside is there. Sometimes it's not. Just remember this: It takes volume (demand) to move a stock a lot higher, but a stock can really just fall of its own weight. It doesn't necessarily take a lot of selling to crush a stock, just a lack of buyers (demand).

TREND KNOCKOUTS

Q: *I remember David Landry referring to a setup by the name of "Trend Knock-Out." What exactly are the rules for this setup and how does it work?*

Answered by Duke Heberlein 2000-09-16

The Trend Knock-Out is a momentum trading strategy that attempts to take advantage of a short-term selloff in an uptrending security and a subsequent reversal. The setup is simple. First, identify a strongly uptrending stock or future as measured by an uptrending ADX reading of 30 or higher, or a stock with a three-month relative strength ranking of 95 or higher. Today (day one) the stock or future must trade under the low of at least the previous two bars on its daily chart, but by the end of the session reverse and close in the top half of its range. The following day (day two) you will enter long if the stock trades above the day-one high. This type of price action (selling off and then reversing direction) many times will shake out the weak traders that dump their positions during the selloff and then clear the way for the stock to trade higher and resume its uptrend.

Q: *Dave Landry writes about a two-bar low in the "When Weak Hands Fall" (Trend Knockouts) trading strategy. Does this have to happen in one trading day, and if not, how many days would be too many?*

Answered by Dave Landry 2001-01-13
Suppose it's Wednesday, (for buys) it must then trade below both Monday and Tuesday's lows. The more lows "taken out," the better. You are just less likely to get filled.

Q: *I read your excellent article on "Trend Knockouts." I have one question I would like you to clarify: If the stock has made a three- or four-bar pullback from high, would I change my entry price to the high of the last low bar, or would I still use the second low-bar high as my entry price?*

Answered by Dave Landry 2001-01-13
You could. Many of my patterns start off as one pattern but end up as more common patterns if they don't trigger immediately. For instance, a Bow Tie or a TKO often becomes a pullback after two to three days of not triggering. Therefore, when this occurs, I trade them in the same manner as I would pull-backs.

GAPS *(See also, Chapter 7, p. 123)*

Q: *Mr. Haggerty, could you talk about how to trade the first half-hour with a stock that gaps open and then continues up, without presenting an opening-reversal entry? Seems like I'm missing out on good opportunities!*

Answered by Kevin Haggerty 2000-03-25
I suggest waiting for the first consolidation or pullback of at least .38.

Q: *I have been very successful buying low and selling high many times, but when the market opens high, (like when Nasdaq opens with a 30–40 point gap), I ei-*

ther stay on the sidelines missing huge moves, or sometimes buy off the top. Interestingly, when I follow my intuition and short this gap, I make quick money but I am also scared to do so. My question is this: When do we use gaps to buy high/sell higher?

Answered by Eddie Kwong 2000-01-22

It is both difficult and scary for traders to buy high and sell higher in a fast-moving market. But you simply have to accept the fact that there are days when the market gets caught in a tornado. In a tornado, stationary objects are pulled loose from their foundations and taken for a ride to unexpected places. The traditional rules and patterns don't apply on those days because they are purely momentum driven. Stocks that are in motion will continue to be so. As for specific parameters for trading gaps, here is what Dave Landry advises:

> Gap openings that I am more inclined to trade occur when market conditions are favorable and the gap isn't too large. "Too large" can be gauged in terms of the volatility of the stock and the pattern (setup) being traded. A two-point gap may be too large for a stock that barely moves two points in a week. On the other hand, a two-point gap for a volatile stock, say one that trades 5–10 points in a day, isn't as significant.

Q: *Do you have any rules for gap openings? In the past, I have had a short list of stocks I would like to buy, but they gap up at the open. Sometimes I have jumped in and watched the stock retrace, fill the gap and end down for the day. Other times I have waited for a retracement that never came, and the stock had a huge day. Is there anything to look for while the gap situation is unfolding that may tip off which way the stock will go?*

Answered by Jeff Cooper 2000-01-15

You have to be careful about chasing pop-up opens even if the stock is in a strong trend. If the trend is down or questionable or choppy, then these may actually be good to short depending on current market dynamics at the time. You must also be careful about chasing stocks on large gaps after a multi-day strong advance. If the stock is coming out of a pullback or in an underlying uptrend or out of a consolidation, it may be worth considering chasing. If I've seen some volume occur before the open, or if there appears to be some meaningful news event, it may also be worth chasing. I won't chase air (i.e., if a big gap occurs with little to no trade). As a rule of thumb, I prefer to wait for an intraday pullback or the first consolidation to get long after a gap. Speculation is observation; you have to observe the behavior. There are no hard and fast rules about gaps. The key is to be flexible and loose as a goose. If the gap is real, they should come back for it either later the same day or within a few days. Sometimes the hardest trade is to not take the trade. Stalking for setups is more rewarding than shooting at anything that moves. Institutions don't need to chase typically, but when they do chase, it does often lead to explosive moves. However, it's not easy to determine whether a big gap is going to lead to that kind of move. If there is persistent buying after the first 15 minutes, it may be a tip-off.

Q: *I have a question regarding gap plays, e.g., IBM gapped down, then moved up slightly and now keeps coming down. Would you still wait for it to clear the first gap's low before entering (since it didn't go further down on the following day)?*

Answered by Loren Fleckenstein 2000-10-28
If the stock doesn't undercut the intraday low of the gap-down day on the very next day, then the low of the gap-down-day low ceases to be the trigger. The short signal comes whenever a stock finally falls below the intraday low of the prior session. In IBM's case, the short signal occurred on Monday Oct. 23, when the stock fell below the Friday Oct. 20 session's low of 94 3/16. Let me illustrate this in the following example.

After warning of lower-than-expected Q3 revenue, Priceline (PCLN) gapped down on Sept. 27 (Point A), closing at 10 3/4. Shares closed up to 11 7/8 on Sept. 28, then traded sideways to close again at 11 7/8 on Sept. 29, setting an intraday low at 11 1/2. A move below that low (Point B) would become your pivot point to short. Priceline complied the next session (Point C).

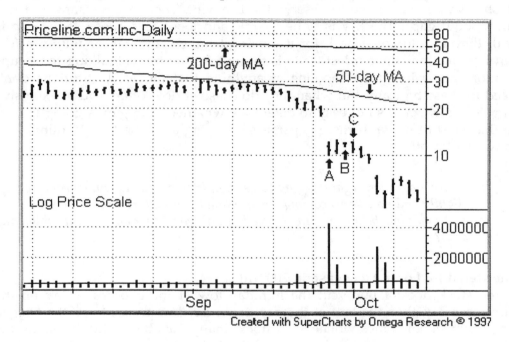

Created with SuperCharts by Omega Research © 1997

Q: *I've found that I labor for hours on setups just to have them nullified by the apparent increase in gapping activity at the open. Any suggestions?*

Answered by Marc Dupée 1999-05-15
Gaps generally express strong market sentiment. If a market gaps, it should continue in the direction of the gap. But if it doesn't, it expresses doubt about the "strength" of that market sentiment and is likely to reverse. So when a market gaps open, but closes weakly, it is saying it wants to fill the gap and go back the other way.

WHIPLASH is a short-term strategy made public by Larry Connors and Linda Raschke in their book *Street Smarts*. It gets you in early on a trade and lets you exploit (weak) market sentiment on opening gaps. Enter the trade market on the close (MOC) to take advantage of the next day's follow-through. Here is the buy setup (sell setups are reversed):

1. The market must gap lower than the previous day's low.

2. The close must be higher than the open and in the top 50% of its daily range.

3. If steps 1 and 2 are met, buy MOC.

4. If the market opens below the close, exit and take a loss.

5. Trail stops.

6. Here is a recent example.

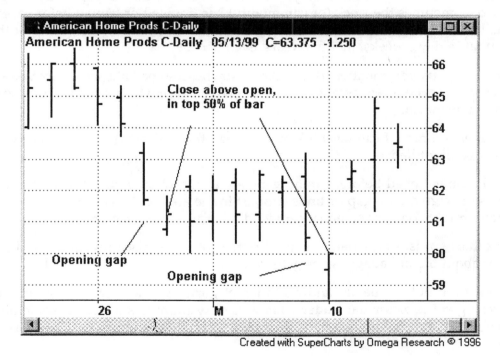

Q: *This is in regard to gaps being filled after a stock or index gaps up or down. For instance, I have been waiting for EMC, YHOO and the COMPX to fill the recent gaps made on June 1 and June 2. Won't they be filled eventually? What's your opinion on noticeable gaps like these? For instance, EMC's gap is the high of 122 on the first and the low made on the second of 126 5/8—pretty big. I hesitate sometimes on recommendations by Kevin and Dave because I see gaps in stocks they are long. Usually, they come back down to fill those gaps. Sometimes, though, I miss opportunities because they don't fill right away, and I miss a good trade. I look forward to your opinion on noticeable gaps like EMC's.*

Answered by Dave Landry 2000-07-08

Gaps *do not* always get filled. I can show you tons of gaps going back 10, 15 and 20 years that have never been filled. I'd even bet that you could find gaps made 100 years ago that have yet to be filled. Also, on the gaps that do get filled, sometimes the stock (or commodity) has doubled or tripled before eventually coming back down and filling the gap. And sometimes the filling of the gap takes days, weeks, months, years, even decades.

Will the gaps you mentioned get filled? Maybe. Maybe later today, maybe tomorrow, maybe a few weeks, maybe a few years, maybe a decade from now. Or maybe never.

So in *my* opinion, I cannot think of a strategy that will work on the premise of gaps getting filled.

As I've mentioned before, I think gaps are a sign of strength. If a market follows through after a gap or finds support in the area of the gap (*not closing it!*), then I might consider an entry, provided other technicals are present.

In other words, I *may* trade in the direction of gaps, place my stops, and not care about the old adage "gaps get filled."

Now, I am not the be-all, know-all market guru. And let's face it: No one is. Every great professional trader I know is very humble and learns something new every day. All traders have their own techniques and beliefs. Therefore, if you believe something about filling gaps that is tradable, then by all means, you should trade it. Even though I think differently. And let's face it: If we all didn't have our different opinions, the markets would not exist.

Q: *I am looking at the chart of VOCL, mentioned in your Feb. 23 "Trading Outlook." What about the gap there between Feb. 1 and Feb. 2? Shouldn't it close before I attempt to go long on the stock? I'd appreciate your opinion, as many times I see a stock I want to go long on, but if I see a gap, I wait because it usually comes back down to close eventually.*

Answered by Dave Landry 2000-03-04
Gaps in direction of the trend are a bullish sign. Notice VocalTec has gapped higher, but so far, has held above the gap (a). This suggests that the stock has the potential to trade higher.

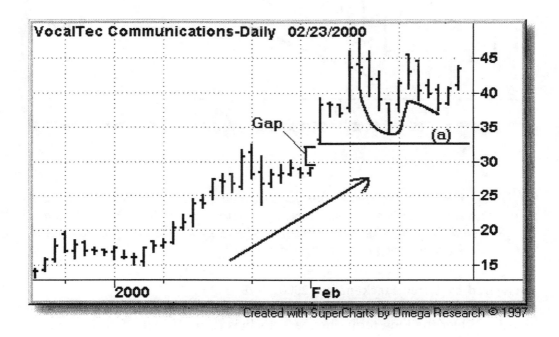

Waiting for gaps to close is a Wall Street myth. Often stocks gap and keep on going. Take a look at Analog Devices (ADI). Notice that it hasn't looked back since gapping higher (a) in a strong uptrend. With the recent strength in the NASDAQ, I'm sure you can find numerous stocks similar to ADI.

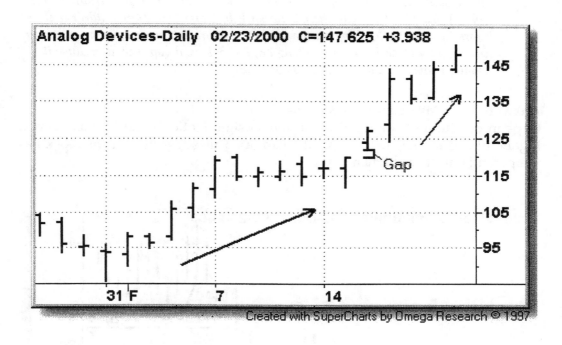

Q: *Hi, Loren. Under what circumstances would you no longer look to short a down gap that had previously met all of your criteria? In other words, when would the pattern no longer be valid? How long do you wait for the stock to break down through the previous day's low?*

Answered by Loren Fleckenstein 2000-11-18
Like most intermediate-term traders, I am more comfortable going long than shorting. Over the long term, the market's bias is up. If I feel that the market is

developing a powerful rally or is nearing a bottom, I would be more reluctant to short a stock. Calling a bottom before a follow-through day is always a dubious enterprise. But as I pointed out with Dell on Nov. 10, we have to start wondering if there's much more bad news for the general market to discount. As a general rule, I also want the gap-down move to come on negative news from the corporation itself rather than analyst downgrades. How many times did we see analysts downgrade great past winners like Dell Computer and Cisco Systems on valuation concerns, only to see those monsters go on to multiply in price? But when the company says "Uncle," you can have more confidence that the company faces real trouble ahead. As for when you short, I personally would short 1/8 below the prior day's low. I also would look to sell and take profits sooner than I would in a long trade.

Q: *My question is about stock graphs and charts. I have three stocks in mind: SCMR, VRTX and ORCH. If you look at their graphs for 7-7-00, you can see that SCMR "gap-opens up" and goes up throughout the day. VRTX "gap-opens up" and goes down. And ORCH "gap-opens up" and goes up after a period of congestion. I bought VRTX, and I was stopped out. My question is this: Just from looking at its graphs and charts, is there any way to tell whether a stock will go up or down after it "gap-opens up"? Or is it just luck?*

Answered by Jeff Cooper 2000-07-15
There really is no definitive answer to your question. The age-old problem has always been when to chase and when to fade gap openings. No one ever knows. You have to just make your decision based on the overall market tone, the tone of the market for the particular day, and the stock's pattern on its chart. There is a big difference, for example, between chasing a gap out of congestion and going after a gap opening on a stock that has run up 20 points within a week. Every stock and every setup is different and must be looked at on an individual basis.

Q: *On March 7, 2000, Procter & Gamble gapped down on the open on earnings disappointment. On March 8, in your commentary you noted that this was the perfect trade because the stock opened near the low of the day. Should we generally be looking to go long big-cap NYSE stocks that gap down if they hold that initial low for the first few bars?*

Answered by Kevin Haggerty 2000-03-25

You buy it at the market on the opening if it is a big-cap stock, and you decide that it is an overdone emotional gap down. Procter & Gamble is a quality stock, and the specialist was taking it down 34%, which I thought was too much and would have a rebound. Each case is different: If it's accounting problems or fraud, don't touch it. These gap indications come across the Dow news wire pre-opening and keep changing as the specialist puts together the buyers and sellers.

RELATIVE STRENGTH

Q: *After running a scan like the 99 12-month, 99 six-month, 99 three-month relative strength scan to find the hottest stocks over the last three-month, six-month and one-year periods, what characteristics, if any, give us a clue as to which stocks will continue to rise and which ones are about to roll over and die?*

Answered by Eddie Kwong 2000-04-22

There are certain telltale signs we look for in a stock with high relative strength that might be vulnerable:

- **The stock is overextended.** That is, the upward momentum of the stock has gotten so out of hand that it has shot up far away from its closest support level. If you see a stock rocketing higher with barely a pause, it is going parabolic. Stocks like these often stall out and plummet back to earth. If, on the other hand, you focus on stocks where support is not too far below your entry point, the severity of any potential decline is likely reduced.

- **The stock is moving higher on light volume.** Volume is what fuels rallies. You need a lot of traders buying into a stock and then holding onto their shares. The flip side would be a more favorable setup, which would occur if you saw a stock exploding higher, accompanied by high volume, followed by a minor pullback on light volume. That would suggest that the traders who bought the stock are holding onto their shares.

- **The stock drops on good news.** Sometimes a stock will look good, but exhibit weakness on what common sense would dictate is good news. When you see a stock tank when it beats earnings estimates, that's not good.

- **Pattern deterioration.** You might see the stock start to form a head and shoulders or double top. While these patterns don't mean much until they're complete, why not steer clear of stocks exhibiting hints of this and stick to those with clean charts?

Q: *For Loren Fleckenstein or Kevin Marder. I bought JNI (JNIC) on Nov. 7. The stock dropped dramatically on Nov. 10. I would like to learn from my mistakes. Could you guide me as to what I did wrong? Was it an error in stock selection, or were there clues technically that I missed, or was it as a result of the general downturn in the market unrelated to JNIC?*

Answered by Loren Fleckenstein 2000-11-25
Since you're addressing your question to Kevin or me, I assume you are an intermediate-term trader. Obviously, I'm looking at the stock with the benefit of hindsight. I would love to tell you that I could have foreseen the selloff subsequent to your Nov. 7 entry, but there's nothing in the chart that would have enabled me to see trouble ahead.

That said, I would definitely NOT have bought JNIC on Nov. 7 for a number of reasons. First, the general market is in terrible shape. Nov. 7 obviously coincided with the election, and the market appeared to be discounting a Bush victory at the time. The subsequent downside, in my view, is due mainly to earnings deceleration, but the presidential chaos served as a good cue to whack a number of stocks. Prior to Nov. 7, however, the market still looked pretty sick. Poor volume, poor action in the indexes and a general scarcity of high-RS stocks completing sound bases. In such conditions, you should stay largely or completely in cash unless you are adept at short-selling.

Second, JNIC itself was already hyperextended by Nov. 7. On Nov. 7, it pulled back slightly after five straight up days. You should buy stocks after they have consolidated recent gains and then break out. When you buy on the breakout, you should catch them as close to the pivot as possible in order to avoid getting into a hyperextended position.

Q: *When I do an RS scan on Ameritrade (AMTD), it shows an RS of 95. This suggests the stock is in an uptrend. Yet when I pull the stock up, it's clearly in a downtrend. Is this number correct?*

CHAPTER 4

Answered by Dave Landry 1999-10-23

Looking to the daily chart of Ameritrade, we see that it is clearly in a down-trend. However, the RS calculation is based on the performance of the last 12 months.

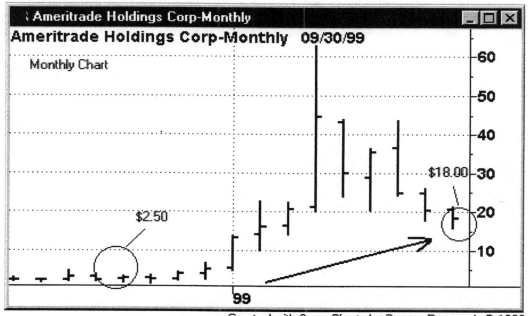

Created with SuperCharts by Omega Research © 1996

Looking at a monthly chart, we see that one year ago it was trading around $2.50 per share. So even with its recent downtrend, at a closing price of around $18, it's still up 720% over the last year—hence, the high-RS reading (95), which suggests it has outperformed 95% of all other stocks.

CHAPTER 5

Daytrading

Daytrading has captured the attention of both the public and the news media during the past few years. The proliferation of and ease of acquiring computerized intraday analysis tools and online trading hookups greatly helped many people to become traders of short-term moves that occur during the course of a single day. While there are many electronically based tactics that are unique to daytrading owing to many order execution scenarios, there is really no difference between the basic patterns, strategies and money-management rules that daytraders follow and those who hold positions days, weeks or months at a time. Success in daytrading, however, hinges upon being able to quickly recognize opportunities and seize upon them without hesitation and curtail losing trades—again, without hesitation.

RISK EXPOSURE

Q: *I have put 10% of my portfolio at risk this year to learn how to trade. I have made about 250 trades this year. So far I'm up 20%, going only long. I use only Level I, live tickers and, recently, live charts. Would you recommend I invest in Level II, ECNs or other tools, including more monitors, etc. for daytrading?*

Answered by Duke Heberlein 2000-10-21

First, let me commend you on showing great discipline in using only a small portion of your capital in your first year while you jump in and learn how to succeed at this game. I have known some traders who have succeeded at trading without Level II. However, it is a handicap to do so, due to the fact that with Level II access, you are able to view who is bidding for stock (buying) and who is offering (selling), as well as at what price, and how much (number of shares) they are looking to either buy or sell. This information is invaluable for the intraday trader, and for some strategies, such as Jeff Cooper's "Stepping In Front Of Size," you will have to have level II access to see the size and price of the bids coming in from the market makers and ECNs.

ENTRY STRATEGIES

Q: *How can I buy a position at 3:30 or so each day and profit from that position the next morning at the open? Is this possible? What am I to look for?*

Answered by Marc Dupée 1999-07-03

Holding positions overnight for liquidation the next morning can be profitable, but it depends on the specific circumstances of any individual trade. One obvious characteristic you might want to look for is a market that seems likely to follow through—perhaps those that close very strongly or weakly.

Of course, the big drawback to holding positions overnight is that you expose yourself to overnight risk—news events that may impact your position adversely when it's difficult or impossible for you to get out of your trade.

For illustration purposes, an approach that enters on the close and exits on the open takes advantage of Larry Connors' CVR IV. It uses the CBOE's VIX (Market Volatility Index) to identify intraday reversals in market sentiment. The intent is to exploit large intraday reversals in the VIX. Lets look at the rules:

If the VIX closes 1.50 or more points greater than its open, sell the S&P futures market-on-close (MOC).

1. Cover your position on the opening the next morning (Globex is omitted).

2. If the VIX closes 1.5 or more below its open, buy the S&P futures MOC.

3. Sell your position on the opening the next morning.

A change of 1.50 in the VIX indicates a major short-term change in sentiment that is carried over into the next morning. The position is not held throughout the day because sentiment changes quickly. This technique can be used in a Friday–Monday system as well. Pay particularly close attention to CVR IV Friday–Monday setups when the VIX reading changes by 2.50 points or more. These trades have a higher success ratio.

Q: *Generally, we enter a stock when the high of the prior day is taken out. In a volatile market like this, do we take the trade even if we get the signal in the first 10 or 15 minutes of trading, or do we wait for a pullback? I would like to know what Jeff Cooper does in his personal trading.*

Answered by Marc Dupée 1999-07-03
Jeff says he will take the first morning breakout if there is a strong setup, but the decision is also based on intuition and knowledge of the stock. He says, "most of the starburst activity is in the first 15 minutes to one hour, and the last hour of trading" and he wants to be on board for big moves.

For instance, if the stock was setting up the night before, pivoting up out of a cup-and-handle pattern or from a pullback, he will trade the first breakout. In other situations, he would be more "leery," wait for a morning pullback and then enter when a stock re-crossed an entry point.

He would not make an early entry if the stock had just run up for multiple days and gapped open above the high.

By contrast, Kevin Haggerty said that he knows traders who make their living fading (trading against) the morning retail-order flow. Kevin advises not to trade between 9:30 and 9:45 ET, because when all the retail orders come through, the "lambs are taken to slaughter."

Depending on the stock, it can be a safer bet to wait until after 9:45, let the stock pull back, and then enter after it re-crosses your level.

SECOND ENTRY

Q: *I want to make sure I understand the second entry correctly. Let's say the ideal entry price is 62 and the price shoots through that price up to 63. Would the second entry be on the way back down through 62 or would it have to go back down and then up again?*

Answered by Kevin Haggerty 2000-11-11
If, for example, the previous day's close was 62 and your entry was 62.125 and you got entry and it went to 62.50. The stock then traded down to 61.50 and you were stopped out, but when it recrossed 62, you took a second entry. There are many times you might wait for the second entry to be your first entry and often the wiggle has been taken out of the stock.

Q: *Jeff Cooper uses the phrase the "second mouse gets the cheese" sometimes in his column. Please explain the reference.*

Answered by Duke Heberlein 2001-01-13
Jeff uses this reference to allude to the second occurrence of an activity, for example, a second entry into a pattern. He wrote, "The index shows a pattern of higher lows and higher highs since late November. In fact, this is the third higher low, suggesting the *second mouse will get the cheese—i.e. this second close over the 50-day moving average should be successful.*"

Q: *What is Kevin Haggerty referring to when he says buy stock on second entry point, and how is that determined?*

Answered by Kevin Haggerty 2000-01-22
In my opinion, second entries are, at times, the better entry. During the first

half-hour of trading, there is often a high level of volatility, as market makers and specialists deal with orders flowing in for a stock. Price swings might cause you to get stopped out of a position, but a disciplined trader will stick to his trading plan and look for another chance to buy back the stock at the same entry price. This is called the second entry.

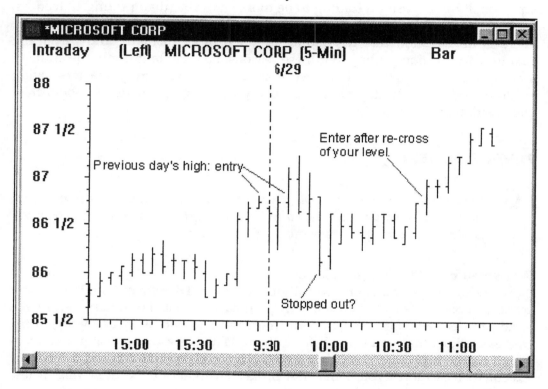

COMPARED TO OTHER TIME FRAMES

Q: *Kevin Marder, I notice you are not a "daytrader." Is this due to circumstances, or do you think daytrading is not the most effective way to make money in the markets? I have found that I have done best when I buy and hold for a week or two. However, I am finding it quite a challenge not to daytrade, with frequent poor results relative to the markets, as well as time lost that could be used elsewhere. I know every trading rule, but cannot control emotions once the bars start "moving."*

Answered by Kevin Marder 2000-05-13
I personally find position trading to be more enjoyable than pulling sixteenths, eighths, quarters, etc., out of the market a number of times each day. As well, there is no question that daytrading is much more mentally and physically taxing than position trading. For these reasons, I am content to ply the strategy I now practice. However, I believe that someone who truly masters swing trading, and possibly daytrading, probably can put up bigger numbers than the position trader in a given year.

DIRECT ACCESS

Q: *I have been trading for a couple of years but am now looking to step up my activity. Is it important to have a direct-access online broker? Or are there other factors that override the importance of direct access?*

Answered by Eddie Kwong 2000-09-16
Most serious day- and short-term traders consider Direct-Access (DA) brokers to be a must. Loren Fleckenstein has pointed out that daytraders—and even swing traders and intermediate-term traders—can gain an edge owing to the fast executions that you can get from them. Whereas a trader using a conventional online brokerage firm may wait a couple of minutes for an order to be executed, it is more typical that DA broker customers have their fills in less than 15 seconds. The elimination of these delays can equate to a significant advantage in execution price to a DA customer in fast-moving markets.

Q: *What is the best way to exit or enter a fast-moving momentum stock? Use a market order with SOES or INCA, or use a limit order plus 1/8 above/below the best bid and ask? Also, which leading indicator is the best to use? Should I use a tech giant like Yahoo or just the Nasdaq futures?*

Answered by Duke Heberlein 2000-07-08

During fast market conditions, if momentum is taking the stock up, the best way to enter a trade is to buy at the market on the SOES. If you use an ECN (such as ARCA), hit it at the ask. If you are going to sell into strength (giving you positive slippage), use the ECN to offer at the asking price. In the case of a stock moving down, you can buy it at the bid using an ECN. If you are selling the stock, hit the bid using either SOES or an ECN.

As for the second part of your question, I would use the Nasdaq futures. One stock would not give you an indicator for the overall market, and it could be subject to pressures on any given day that have nothing to do with your trading.

Q: *Could someone please explain to me the difference between a "direct-access" broker and an online broker? Both seem to use the Internet, but I gather that they handle orders very differently. I understand direct access is used a lot by daytraders. Why would a daytrader use a direct-access broker instead of trading out of one of the daytrading centers?*

Answered by Dave Landry 2000-07-08

With direct access, your order is routed directly to an ECN or an exchange. With an online brokerage, your order gets sent to a broker. In some cases, your order is simply an e-mail to the broker. The broker then executes your order where he sees fit. Therefore, with direct access, you essentially eliminate the middle man. Is it necessary? It depends on your trading style. If you are a position trader, then the executions are not as crucial to your long-term success. But if you are a daytrader making numerous trades, then direct access becomes a must.

In regards to the daytrading centers, many of these centers market themselves as providing the best hardware, data feeds, telecommunications, and other equipment needed for daytrading. They also supply some sort of direct-access trading platform. To use all this, you pay a monthly fee. In addition, the centers make commissions from your trades.

If you want to daytrade from your home or office, you should make sure you have the best equipment you can afford and have a direct-access broker.

Why choose a daytrading center over your home or office? I suppose some choose to go to a center to avoid having to install and maintain the equipment necessary. Also, some prefer the company of other traders when trading. Others prefer to trade in a vacuum.

LEVEL II TRADING

Q: *Could someone please tell me what the term "Nasdaq Level II" means? It is usually used in connection with quotes.*

Answered by Duke Heberlein 2000-05-20
Nasdaq Level II is a quote screen that gives the most current quotes and the size of those quotes (number of shares bought or sold) for each market maker trading a particular stock.

The Level II screen has two sides: On the left side are the listed market makers and their bids; on the right side are the listed market makers and their offers, or asking prices.

All of the bids and offers shown on the quote screen are displayed, along with the number of shares that each market maker must buy or sell at that price. The highest-priced bid and the highest-priced offer are referred to as the inside market. This is usually—but not always—the "real-time" quote that you get from Web sites or from retail quote services.

The advantage a trader gets from viewing the Level II screen is that it allows him or her to see all of the available bids and offers for a stock, just like the professionals do. The market makers in Level II have no place to hide from the traders at home or in the trading rooms. If Goldman Sachs is selling a stock, it will show by their low offer on the screen; and if Morgan Stanley is a heavy buyer, it will show up by the increases in the price of their bids. Therefore, Level II is a most useful tool for the short-term trader.

Q: *Would someone be willing to go into a lengthy discussion of the importance of watching the size of the bid/ask?*

Answered by Eddie Kwong 2000-07-01
While monitoring the bid/ask is far from mandatory, properly applied it can give you an edge. How significant that edge is, however, depends on what trading strategy you're already using. If you're a position trader looking to buy quality companies breaking from bases, then looking at the bid/ask isn't really all that relevant to you. But if you want to refine your decision making, for very short-term trades, it can help to know when institutional traders are bidding or asking in large size blocks. The finer nuances of exploiting this is a Jeff Cooper strategy known as "Stepping In Front Of Size." Here's how it works theoretically. When a big bid comes in and is executed in a thinly traded stock, it'll usually drive the price of the stock up a bit. If you see a size bidder, you can place an order that is an eighth above his bid. When his order gets executed, the price shoots up, and you go for a ride. Please be aware that this is a very condensed version of the strategy. If you're interested knowing more, check out Jeff Cooper's *Hit and Run* books.

Q: *For Duke Heberlein: I've enjoyed your lessons on Level II trading. Do you see market makers like Goldman Sachs using the INCA and ISLD ECNs to disguise their intentions? It seems to me that ECN activity is increasing greatly, while daytrading activity seems to be decreasing. This would seem to indicate that market makers moving quantity aren't showing their names as much, and are using ECNs. Your thoughts would be appreciated.*

Answered by Duke Heberlein 2000-12-16
I'm not sure that daytrading activity really is decreasing, but you are correct in your observation: Large market makers often do route large orders in blocks through ECNs.

What you will want to look for are increasing bids (or, in the case of selling, decreasing offers) of sizable volume, via the ECN, that are either at the inside bid, or possibly at the second price level. This is not as reliable as spotting the market maker itself in such activity, but it could be an indication of an institution with a sizable order to fill.

For example, let's say that Goldman Sachs (GSCO) is sitting on the inside bid all day, bidding sizes of 500 to 1,000 shares that are, according to time-and-sales screens, getting filled. Then GSCO disappears, and a large block is bid on INCA and is filled on time and sales. You can assume that this is most likely GSCO trying to cover up its buying.

While this is not always true, many times it is the case and is a game that institutions are playing in order to throw you off the trail. Institutions will also use this method to appear to be buying as GSCO while they are selling via an ECN.

Q: *I have trouble deciphering the Nasdaq Level II screen. Sometimes the ask side is very heavy, but the stock continues going up for quite a while, even when the bid side is very light. I daytrade and usually think about getting out when this happens. Also, I sometimes have trouble getting into a stock. What do you do when the bid and ask are moving so fast you don't have the time to click your price, then click transmit to even put your order in? By the time you do this, the price is way over you. Do you ever put it in for market or do you pass?*

Answered by Duke Heberlein 2000-08-12
One reason you could be seeing the price continue to rise when the ask side is very heavy and the bids are light on the Level II screen is that the ECNs could be having trouble with their data transmission. Always be sure to check the time and sales along with the bid/ask screen to make sure that it is not simply a lag in data. If it is not, it could be a bullish sign, if buyers are snapping it up when selling is heavy. Regarding your question on order entry, if you are willing to take the trade at 1/8 to 1/4 above the inside ask, place a buy stop at this level above the inside ask. This will place your order in line, and if it is not hit, there is no trade.

In a fast-moving momentum stock, this is really the only way to keep the price from moving away from you and chasing the stock. In a fast-moving stock, however, it could still overshoot your bid, and sometimes it is simply best to avoid these stocks if you've missed this opportunity and go on to the others you are following on your screen.

Q: *I've noticed while watching Level II action that often INCA will sit on the bid, accumulating stock. They will show they want to buy 1,000 shares; a print will go by for (let's say) 800 shares; and then I will see INCA showing they want to buy only 200 shares. A few moments later, the bid will be refreshed to 1,000 shares. If instead of INCA, however, you have a market maker like PIPR, the same thing happens, except that the bid never changes or gets refreshed. So does a market maker not have to refresh his bid when he gets hit (buys the stock when sitting on the bid)? And can the market maker buy a larger amount of stock than he's showing he wants to buy on Level II?*

Answered by Duke Heberlein 2000-05-06
The market makers do refresh their bids. It happens electronically, and many times you may not see the change. Market makers don't have to change the prices of their bids until another market maker outbids them. Remember that all market makers are competing against each other, and also against all other traders.

Market makers can buy more shares than they are showing on the Level II screen. They are required only to buy at least the number of shares they have bid on. This is why you can see 500 shares traded to a market maker whose posted bid had been only 200 shares.

Q: *For Kevin Haggerty, do you find it helpful to use Level II or order-book information during the day, or do you trade strictly off of the charts? Also, if the QQQs or SPYs finish at the low for the day, and open flat to lower the next day, how do you determine a continuation entry (i.e., without a wide-ranging bar)?*

Answered by Kevin Haggerty 2000-05-20
To answer the first part of your question, yes, I do find Level II helpful to determine liquidity, but I prefer the big-cap stocks that all trade tight. I also use

Level II to see which firms are active and if there is a dominant side (which usually means an institutional order is working).

As for the second part of your question, I use the five-minute charts and look for a reversal pattern, such as trading above the high of the third-lower high if the market dynamics are looking good.

CANDLESTICKS

 Q: *I have been using candlestick charts for intraday trading on a three-minute time frame. What confirming indicators should I use with them? Or is there a better method?*

Answered by Tsutae Kamada 2000-10-28
Use candlesticks with trendlines, moving averages and oscillators, such as stochastics and momentum indicators. Try to get as many confirmations as possible before you trade.

CHAPTER 6

Shorting

Shorting is a strategy unto itself for three reasons:

1. *The market tends to behave very differently when going down than when going up.*

2. *When selling short, your trade won't be executed until the next uptick.*

3. *The stock market in the long run has an inherent upward bias.*

The art of selling short and the rewards that follow have attracted a devoted following of traders due to the fact that you can often make money faster by shorting than you can going long. The market tends to lose ground faster when a strong downtrend takes hold than it gains when a strong uptrend is in place. A graphic case in point is the action in the Nasdaq during the year 2000. The Nasdaq took over 10 years to reach 5000. It took only one year for that gain to get chopped in half. Individual stocks within the Nasdaq suffered rapid losses of an equal or worse degree. Panic and fear tend to drive traders and investors to sharper extremes of selling behavior than is the case with greed and optimism's stimulation of buying behavior.

The caveat is that short-selling is harder to do than trading on the long side. In fact, some professional traders are selling short only under special circumstances because of its unique challenges. This is the case even in bear markets. Down moves in the market tend to be sharp, dramatic, and over with quickly. You've probably heard of short-covering rallies. A market will plunge for short periods of time, but then stage dramatic, sustained rallies. These rallies are often fueled by amateur short-sellers who were quick enough and who are panicked out of their short positions.

All this said, short-selling is an important skill to learn because bear markets do happen. Great opportunities occur on the short-side. If you want to succeed over the long-term as a trader, knowing how to trade both sides of the market is important. Many new traders and investors were attracted into the business during the great bull market of the late 1990s. They learned strategies that worked great during that time. And they lost big when the market went into a bearish phase in 2000. Not only that, but they missed many opportunities to profit on the short side. If you don't know the basics of short-selling, learn them.

THE BASICS

Q: *Could you explain selling short to me? I know it is when you sell a stock at a higher price believing it will decline and then buying it at a lower price to make a profit. But I need to know some particulars of this trade. Is it more risky? Are there any special requirements one must meet in order to sell short?*

Answered by Sterling Ten 2000-08-26
Shorting is generally considered more risky because of the risk-and-reward factor. Consider this: In the case of buying a stock, your maximum risk is the price of the stock and the reward may be infinite. For example, when you buy a stock at $10, your maximum loss will be $10, but there's no telling how much higher the stock can go, thus, the reward may be infinite. On the other hand, shorting the stock is the total opposite. Your maximum return is the price of the stock, but your risk in unlimited. Thus, it is more important to

have a stop loss when shorting. In order to be able to sell short, you must have a margin account, since you are borrowing the stock from the brokerage. Your brokerage must have the shares available for you to short a particular stock, and the stock cannot be in a downtick.

Q: *I continue to read articles from Dave Landry and others about how you should play both sides of the market. I tend to play breakouts to new highs or lows. However, on the short side, it seems like if it's a good short, the price travels too far away from the downside breakout before an uptick occurs. Of course, this is not a problem on the upside. Any ideas on how to deal with this problem?*

Answered by Dave Landry 1999-10-02

As a trader, I believe in free markets. In my opinion, the uptick rule for stocks (there is no uptick rule in futures) is one more regulation that reduces market freedom. Your observation is correct: Stocks can get away from you on the short side if they don't uptick. In general, less liquid stocks and more volatile stocks tend to move further without an uptick. Therefore, if you are having problems getting your shorts off (no pun intended), you might try to focus on more liquid or less volatile stocks—or change your methodology for thinly traded and volatile stocks. For example, you might find it easier to enter on a pullback instead of a breakout in these stocks. Even though shorting stocks does have its pitfalls, you must make it part of your trading regimen to survive in the markets long term.

Q: *David Landry, I have read your informative article on short selling, and am interested in shorting stocks. However, I am concerned about the part where you say, "should the stocks begin to rise, you would have to add more money to your account (or exit the position)." If in the remote instance where the price of the stock gaps up way past the stop-buy level and there's not enough money in the account to cover the gap in price, does it mean that I'll need to meet a margin call? What if I don't have enough money to meet a margin call? What about dividends? You don't touch on that in the article. If I am shorting a particular stock and the company pays out dividends, is my ac-*

count debited for the amount of dividend paid out? I was warned that, and I quote, "short selling should be left only to the professionals, as theoretically, your losses could be unlimited." I thought that if I have stop-losses in place, the worst-case scenario wouldn't be too far from my bail-out plan. I would appreciate your feedback.

Answered by David Landry 2000-01-22

Congratulations for making the effort to learn how to short. Yes, it is a little more complicated that simply going long. However, if you want to make a long-term living trading the stock market, you should learn how to play both sides of the market. This bull market has made a lot of people successful "traders," but will they be around through the next correction? The next bear market? Doubtful.

Regarding gaps, if the stock gaps higher and you don't have enough money in your account to cover your losses, you will receive a margin call. If you fail to meet the margin call, your broker (by law) is required to close out your position. In reality, you should be adequately capitalized because sooner or later, you will likely experience positions (either long or short!) that will go sharply against you overnight (or even intraday if a stock is halted, pending news, and then subsequently gaps). Hopefully, through consistent disciplined trading, you'll make enough on your winners to cover such events. Regarding your question, you had a stop order in and the market traded through the order. The order would get executed (because your stop was hit) and you would owe the broker any balance. As far as dividends, yes, you are responsible. However, think about what a dividend is. A dividend is essentially a company giving the shareholder a piece of the company. So in many cases, this dilution of the company (from the stock to the shareholder) will cause the stock to drop by the amount of the dividend. So, it's possible that the dividend of a stock that you are short will take care of itself.

As far as "unlimited" losses . . . yes, you could theoretically lose an "unlimited" amount of money. Suppose you shorted Microsoft 10 years ago and were still short? Each month (week or day!) your broker would call and ask for more money. Now, who in their right mind would continue to add money to their account? So yes, "theoretically" you could lose an unlimited amount of money. **However, through controlling losses and following a disciplined trading plan, shorting can be a valuable tool to add to your arsenal.**

Q: *I am setting up my charts with the RS (relative strength) on them. Could you please tell me the parameters you use for shorting?*

Answered by Mark Boucher 2000-03-04

When selling short, look for stocks that have made new lows and are ranked in the bottom 15%–20% of both relative strength (RS) and earnings (ER). Because they have such weak fundamental and technical characteristics, they have the best chance to move significantly lower. Shorts should be taken only in stocks meeting our down-fuel criteria that have valid breakdowns of four-plus-week flags or cup-and-handles on the downside.

Q: *It has been suggested as a short-term trader that I "play" both sides of the market. While I am able to go short and long in my brokerage account, in my IRA I can only go long and buy options. My questions: 1) Which is more advantageous: shorting or buying puts? 2) Since I cannot short in my IRA, what type of options would you suggest would be best to have in a down market?*

Answered by Tsutae Kamada 2000-09-23

Short-selling stocks are high-risk transactions. Your potential gain is limited, but your potential loss is unlimited. You can control this unfavorable risk by purchasing put options. Buying puts requires only a fraction of the money you need for selling stocks short.

In a down market, some investors buy OEX (S&P 100 Index) put options to protect their accounts. But if you have only two or three stocks in your account, you may consider purchasing equity put options for each stock.

Q: *I've noticed a large number of recent IPOs that have sunk below their initial offering prices. I am having a hard time resisting the temptation to short some that have been drowning below that support level for weeks or longer. Is there* *any reason not to jump on them? Most of them are now at the $5 level, but several have a way to go from around $20. My reasoning is that once they go as much as 5 points below, there are no technical reasons for them to defy gravity—especially when their charts indicate strong (though often slow) downward trends.*

Answered by Loren Fleckenstein 2000-06-03

Yes, you can short stocks after they break below their offers. In fact, some rally back toward their offering price, only to stall below it and roll over. It's not hard, of course, to find stocks in downtrends. The key is to time your entry to minimize your chance of getting stopped out and to maximize the odds of a stock heading south after you short. One signal to look for is stocks that make a new low, then pull back. TradingMarkets compiles a list of such stocks after each market close. Click on the Indicators tab near the top of the home page, and then choose the "Pullbacks From Lows" link.

Q: *I'm confidently 100% in cash at the moment, and happy that I have been for the last couple of weeks. My priorities now are taxes, spring cleaning, wind-surfing, and re-reading your courses for the next time around. I have a couple of quick questions: (1) Do intermediate-term momentum traders sell short? (2) The markets seem to continue diverging. With the Dow on what seems to be a solid trend past its own follow-through day, should we consider picking up a few Dow stocks on breakouts?*

Answered by Kevin N. Marder 2000-05-06

I don't sell short, but I know of some intermediate traders who do. Since fear is a more intense emotion than greed, and since fear is the emotion that drives stocks lower, stocks tend to drop faster than they rise. For this reason, the short-seller's timing must be much more precise, making it more difficult to profit from the short side. My suggestion is to paper-trade before you actually try any short sales.

As for your question on buying Dow stocks, I suggest that you concentrate on each stock as an individual entity unto itself, rather than on whether it's part of this index or that index. For example, the Dow has some techs in it, but it also has some industrial names, such as International Paper and Du Pont. Make sure you understand that industrial stocks don't trend as consistently as growth stocks, nor do they appreciate as fast.

MECHANICAL CONSIDERATIONS

Q: *I dug, and searched, and filtered, and plotted, and eventually found several viable short-sale candidates. Expansion Breakdowns, even, hurray! However, when I tried to take a position, five out of six were listed by my broker as "not available for short sale." Can you explain why this happens?*

Answered by Dave Landry 1999-12-04
In all likelihood, these were probably thin issues with very little float. I'd bet that if you were trying to short IBM, Microsoft, General Motors, etc. that the shares would be available. By the way, even if shares are available on a thinner issue, you should always check with your broker to make sure they aren't on the "hard to borrow" list. Otherwise, you could get caught in what is known as a short squeeze where prices are driven higher and you are forced to cover your position.

Q: *Under what circumstances would you no longer look to short a down gap that had previously met all of your criteria? In other words, when would the pattern no longer be valid? How long do you wait for the stock to break down through the previous day's low?*

Answered by Loren Fleckenstein 2000-11-18
Like most intermediate-term traders, I am more comfortable going long than shorting. Over the long term, the market's bias is up. If I feel that the market is developing a powerful rally or is nearing a bottom, I would be more reluctant to short a stock. Calling a bottom before a follow-through day is always a dubious enterprise. But as I pointed out with Dell on Nov. 10, we have to start wondering if there's much more bad news for the general market to discount.

As a general rule, I also want the gap-down move to come on negative news from the corporation itself rather than analyst downgrades. How many times did we see analysts downgrade great past winners like Dell Computer and Cisco Systems on valuation concerns, only to see those monsters go on to multiply in price? But when the company says "Uncle," you can have more confidence that the company faces real trouble ahead. As for when you short, I personally would short 1/8 below the prior day's low. I also would look to sell and take profits sooner than I would in a long trade.

CHAPTER 7

Pattern Setups

In your toolbox at home, you could probably throw away 90% of what's there and still get most major home-improvement or repair tasks done around the house. Give me a screwdriver, hammer and a pair of pliers and I can get the job done.

I suspect that many professional traders view pattern setups the same way. Consisting of little more than a series of specific relationships between data points on a bar chart, good patterns go a long way toward helping traders identifying good trading opportunities. The data points usually consist of some combination that includes the following:

- Open

- High

- Low

- Close

- Intraday range

- Volume

Traders look for specific patterns that consist of a series of these data points over time. Once found, these patterns are usually combined with "big picture" factors such as relative strength, market dynamics (or weakness) and trend. Traders are constantly looking for situations where all the pieces of the puzzle fit together. Consistently profitable traders have the discipline to reject setups where there are missing pieces and pounce on those where all the pieces fall together—without hesitation.

Bear in mind that there is an art to recognizing trading opportunities using the patterns you see on a chart. Every pattern-oriented trader I have ever met identifies their favorite patterns by scanning through charts (paper or computer) the old fashioned way—they look at and analyze them with their own eyes. Developing the skill over time—often a few years—traders are able to sift out the best trades. Pattern-screening tools are available and they can save a tremendous amount of time, but ultimately, when the big buy/sell decisions are made, there is no substitute for the computer that resides between the ears.

ABOUT PATTERNS IN GENERAL

Q: *Where can I learn what the term "pattern setup" means? I am not able to spend hours searching, so I would appreciate the guidance.*

Answered by Marc Dupée 2000-02-05
Stocks trace out chart patterns, many of which repeat. Some charts' price patterns have a high degree of correlation with the future movement of a stock, and when stocks trace out familiar patterns that are likely to repeat, we say the stocks are "set up." Entire books are written on interpreting chart patterns using such names as head-and-shoulders, triangles, pennants, wedges, double- and triple-tops, etc. Momentum traders look for a variety of set up patterns, but one of the better-known ones is the cup-and-handle. TradingMarkets.com screens thousands of stocks set up in this pattern and you can find them on the cup-and-handle-patterns page. Momentum stocks in continuation "pattern setups" have usually made new highs and are expected to keep making new highs. Good screening tools for finding stocks that have shown strong recent price growth or that have hit new highs and could continue higher are the Proprietary Momentum List and the New 60-Day On Double Volume List.

Q: *My question is about the accuracy of chart patterns such as "cup-and-han-dles," "flags" and "triangles." Has any research been done to back-test the accuracy rate of these patterns? If so, which patterns are the most reliable? In my own limited trading experience, I've found the channel or base breakout to be the most reliable.*

Answered by Dave Landry 2000-05-13
Patterns such as cup-and-handles, flags and triangles are discretionary patterns. You (or others) may not agree with what I dub a cup-and-handle or a flag. Therefore, it is difficult to truly quantify such patterns. Some studies have done pattern recognition in an attempt to answer questions like yours. See *The Encyclopedia of Trading Strategies.*

Keep in mind, however, that unless the authors give you the code they use to quantify a pattern, the way they define that pattern may be different from how you define it.

I would recommend that you find patterns you are comfortable with and stick to them. From your question, it seems that you have already done this.

I would then study additional patterns—such as cup-and-handles—but learn to look for the "best" patterns that fit your trading style. After some experience, you'll get a feel for which ones work and which ones don't.

BLOW-OFF TOP

Q: *Please explain the blow-off top.*

Answered by Loren Fleckenstein 2000-01-29
Traders have coined several terms to describe a periodic phenomenon in the stock market: A rising stock suddenly going into an accelerated advance, then sharply turning tail and breaking apart. In addition to blow-off moves, there are climax runs and parabolic moves. The idea is the same. A stock that has already made a long advance suddenly explodes into an extremely sharp ascent. This is synonymous with crowd frenzy. Institutions sell into this move. By the time

they've liquidated their positions, demand dries up, and the stock is up in thin air with no support. In such cases, a stock will often rise 50% or more in a few weeks or days. Then it will make the biggest advance of the blow-off move before reversing course. It's important, though, to discriminate between stocks that enter such sharp advances after long climbs and stocks that explode out of sound price bases. The former were probably already extended. The latter may be showing true strength and worth holding if you're a position trader.

Q: *Do you short climax tops after they confirm a downtrend? It seems like a wonderful short opportunity because of the precipitous plunge that might be involved.*

Answered by Loren Fleckenstein 2000-09-09

I won't tell you it can't be done. I know at least one successful intermediate-term trader who shorts off apparent climax tops and has done well by this tactic. But the volatilities involved are extraordinary. You can get your head handed to you if you aren't able to cover your short quickly. Greg Kuhn and I recently corresponded on this same topic. I'll share with you Greg's view on attempting to short climax tops:

> In my experience, shorting into a climax top can be quite dangerous. How can one know when the final peak is definitely in, other than waiting for the first break? Then again, after that first break, any whipsaw move back up will certainly stop one out of the position. The main rule here, I believe, is a sell rule for a long position doesn't necessarily make a sound short-sale rule.

Q: *Greg Kuhn, can you give an example of a stock that you sold because you thought it was in a climax run, only to find out that it really wasn't? Is this common?*

Answered by Greg Kuhn 2000-06-03

Great question. Take a look at Infospace (INSP) in Q4 of '99. I sold it for a 100%-plus gain in early December, above the 40 area (split-adjusted). I reasoned that I could come back in on it if a major move continued off another five-week-plus basing pattern. Unfortunately, I just watched it go up another

200% over the next three months without me. However, this was extremely unusual and a microcosm of the speculative binge the Naz was under during that period. I've never seen this before during the past 12 years.

In hindsight, I suppose I could have waited for it to at least decisively break its 21-day moving average, which it never did all the way up. This would be one way to stay with a position to confirm that a move is really over. Then again, you risk giving back 20 to 30 percentage points in waiting for confirmation. Since this situation was extremely rare, I suppose if I had to do it over again, I would play it the same way.

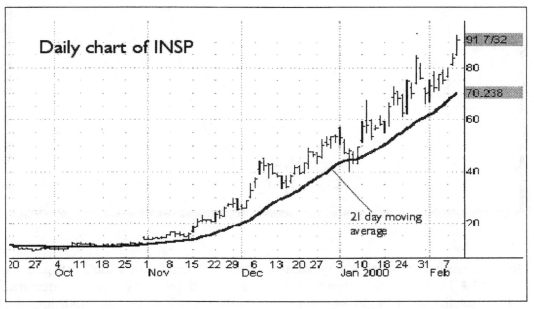

Source: Qcharts.

Q: *Can you please explain parabolic moves?*

Answered by Dave Landry 1999-10-23
A parabolic move, also known as a blow-off top, occurs when a market makes

a large, fast move—rising or falling at an accelerated rate—taking the form of a parabola.

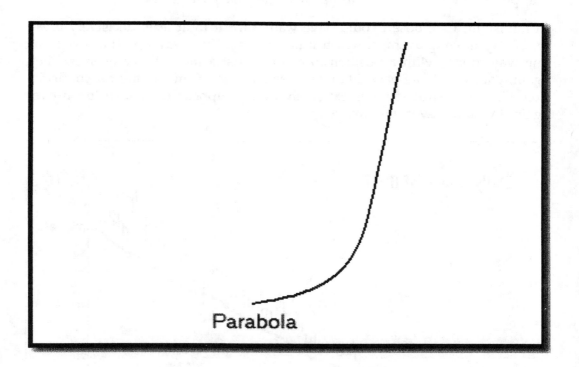

Parabola

Take December '99 coffee, for example. Recently, the futures took off, gaining over 40% in a few days. Such moves are caused by some sort of euphoria, where participants begin to "dog pile" into a market. In commodities, this kind of activity can be triggered by a crop freeze, a war that could disrupt free trade (e.g., the Gulf War), and so on. In stocks, these moves can result from buy-out rumors, enthusiasm over a company's prospects (a new drug, a great product), and so on.

CHAPTER 7

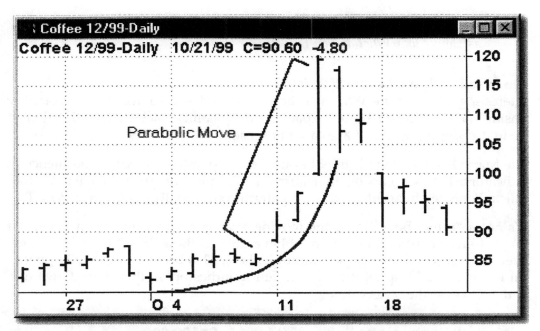

Source: TradeStation by Omega Research.

If you are lucky enough to catch a parabolic move, you should lock in at least part of your profits and tighten your stops on the remaining position because these moves are often short-lived; reality eventually sets in. Referring again to the coffee example, notice that nearly all of the gains were wiped out over the next few days.

BOW TIE

Q: *Your lesson on the Bow Tie pattern is fantastic! Thanks so much for research-ing and sharing your results with us. I am getting wonderful results with Bow Tie applications. I notice, however, that there were stocks that began to form a Bow Tie, but instead of making a lower low on days 2–4, they made an inside-day bar. Then they took off like fireworks! Please look at the chart of Marvell Technology Group (MRVL) since 8/25/00, as an example. I think we can trade with an inside day instead of a lower low, i.e., treating the prior day as "lower low. What do you think?*

Answered by Dave Landry 2000-09-23

Interesting observation. What you have observed is a contraction in volatility (inside days) followed by an expansion of volatility back in the direction of trend. Conceptually, this makes a lot of sense.

The Marvell Technology [MRVL] example you pointed out has a confluence of indicators. It has a cup (a) that forms a mini-pennant (b) (what Jeff Cooper calls a Boomer). In addition, it has a pattern conceptually similar to a Bow Tie.

It's not a "pure" Bow Tie, as the moving averages spread out from being flat (c) vs. from downtrend to uptrend. I have dubbed these "half" Bow Ties. However, as mentioned above, the concept is there. This becomes especially powerful when you add up all the other technical indicators in this chart. Great eye, and thanks for the observation!

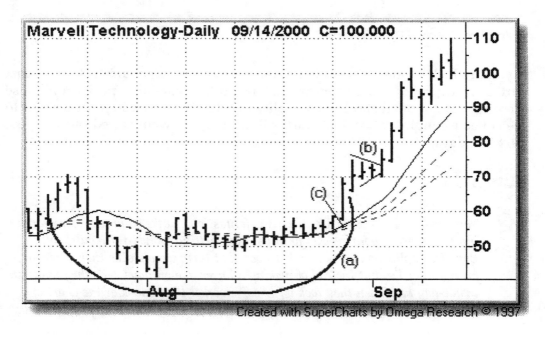

CHAPTER 7

Q: *Once you see a Bow Tie, does it matter how many days it takes before you get your lower low or higher high? I play ABCs and the first entry may be a week or more, but they seem to work. They seem to coincide with the 38% retracement or less. Am I on the right track?*

Answered by Dave Landry 2000-09-30
My original intent was to catch markets soon after they rolled over. Sometimes, however, markets are so strong (weak) that they go weeks without making a lower low (higher high). Ideally, I like to see the stock make a lower low (or higher high for shorts) within one to two weeks after the Bow Tie is formed. The stock is probably still worth playing even if it goes longer than two weeks, but you might want to treat it as you would any other momentum play (i.e., a pullback). In other words, you might want to wait for more than a one-bar correction, as the stock is probably extended at this juncture.

Q: *Has your Bow Tie principle been applied to the market during various times of the year? For example, does it work better in the winter or summer?*

Answered by Dave Landry 2000-09-23
I assume that you are referring to commodities and seasonals. I'm not a big fan of trading seasonals, but there are traders that use them in their analysis. I think the best trades would likely be counter-seasonal with the Bow Tie (or any pattern for that matter). For instance, if a market should be going down because of a seasonal, but instead is going up, then that might offer the most opportunity. Why? Markets often make their biggest moves when they do what they shouldn't.

CUP-AND-HANDLES *(See also, Chapter 3, Intermediate-Term Trading, page 57)*

Q: *What is the definition of a "high-level" cup-and-handle and a "low-level" cup-and-handle?*

Answered by Dave Landry 2000-09-30
Cup-and-handles that form while a stock is bottoming are considered

"low-level." However, sometimes stocks are so strong that they form cup-and-handles within a bigger-picture trend. For instance, I have dubbed a cup-and-handle that forms above the 50-day moving average a "Running Cup-and-Handle." The stock continues to run while the pattern is formed. In other words, it forms a cup-and-handle at high levels.

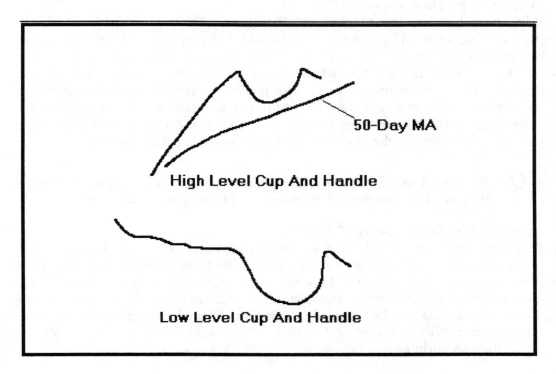

50-Day MA

High Level Cup And Handle

Low Level Cup And Handle

Q: *How can I tell good cup-and-handle patterns from the bad?*

Answered by Loren Fleckenstein 2000-02-26
The cup-and-handle pattern is a continuation pattern. It enables the trader to time when to climb aboard an upward-trending stock by waiting for it to correct, then pouncing at just the right moment after the stock has at least partially recovered.

For starters, go to the authority on this bullish pattern: Bill O'Neil, a legendary trader, founder of *Investor's Business Daily* and author of *How to Make Money in Stocks*, which not only explains this and other bullish patterns, but also how to use them in conjunction with general market analysis and proper stock selection based on fundamental, as well as technical, criteria. Also check out Dave Landry's piece, "Trading with Cup-and-Handle Patterns," in the Stocks/Education section of TradingMarkets.com.

Now here are a few pointers on cup-and-handle patterns: 1) The cup portion should be rounded, not V-shaped, as these sharp recoveries tend to leave the stock overextended even before it reaches new high ground and ripe for a pullback. 2) The handle should slope downward. Upward-sloping handles are failure prone. 3) The handle should form in the upper half of the cup. The dividing line is the mid-range point between the stock's pre-correction intraday high and its intraday low. 4) Volume should dry up in the handle, a sign that selling has abated, setting the stock up for a breakout once strong demand comes to market. 5) The handle should form above the stock's 200-day moving average. 6) Avoid short bases. You need time as well as price declines to shake out weak holders. Look for seven weeks or longer in most cases. Remember also that even sound-looking bases can fail you if you don't play them properly. I think many beginning traders fail to act quickly. So when a stock breaks out of a cup-and-handle base, they chase it after the share price has extended too far. Enter your order the instant the stock exceeds the high of the handle by 1/8 of a point and the move comes on strong volume.

Q: *I've been studying cup-and-handle patterns. What is the average amount of time that a cup takes to form? And what sort of time frame does a handle form within?*

Answered by Kevin N. Marder 1999-11-27
The cup-and-handle pattern can form in any time frame, and on charts ranging from tick bars to monthly bars. Just last Wednesday afternoon (Nov. 24), for example, I noticed it on five-minute bars of the DJIA. It's perhaps most commonly used in equity trading, where many leading stocks will recover from an intermediate-term general market correction of, say, 8% to 12%, by

forming the right side of the cup. Traders, given their varying time frames, look for different things when it comes to the actual size of the cup or handle. For instance, Dave Landry, TradingMarkets.com's director of research, has studied this pattern considerably. His findings, however, may differ a bit from my own.

In my experience, the cup should be a few months in duration, with the handle extending for about two to three weeks. The trough of the handle should extend no more than 15% from the absolute peak of the handle, and ideally, just 10% to 12%. The volume should dry up in the handle, suggesting little profit-taking following the advance associated with the right side of the cup. But these are just general parameters. At the outset of a fresh stock market advance, many leaders will spend a week or less forming the handle before bolting for a big gain.

Q: *What techniques do you use to find stocks that are building solid cup/handle and other solid basing patterns while they are actually building these patterns and prior to the completion of their pre-explosion formations? It seems much easier to filter for stocks that are building short-term trading patterns that have more defined parameters that can be more easily identified with software commands. How do you sort for the intermediate-term prospects?*

Answered by Greg Kuhn 2000-03-25

Initially, I studied Bill O'Neil's model chart patterns—hundreds of them—until I could create the right image in my neural network (a.k.a.—brain). I began 12 years ago with a subscription to *Daily Graphs* and would painstakingly go through each price chart in the NYSE and OTC/AMEX chart books. This literally took me four hours. Today, I have the basic chart patterns—cup/handle, flat base and double bottom—so ingrained in my head that I now peruse the same *Daily Graphs* in less then 30 minutes—3,000 stocks. The patterns I'm looking for stand out like sore thumbs. The stocks that appear to be building bases I keep an eye on each day, watching to see if the right pattern actually develops.

Frankly, I know of some programs that attempt to screen for these patterns, but the parameters have to be kept so loose that it's actually easier to do it by scanning the chart books. There are so many little nuances and slight variations—slight enough to be missed in a loosely defined software program—that they must be picked and studied by the naked eye in my experience. Like any software program, if the parameters are too strict, too many stocks miss the "cut."

Without sounding arrogant, there is nothing, absolutely nothing easy about investing in the stock market. Bottom line: It takes time, a lot of time, practice, and mistakes. But like anything worthwhile in life, the most difficult things are the most rewarding.

Q: *Greg, regarding breakouts from cup-and-handle patterns: If a stock breaks out and on the same day drops and closes below the pivot point, can you now use the intraday high on this failed attempt as a new pivot point and wait for another five-day-plus handle to form? Or would you rather wait for the stock to further advance up the right side past that new pivot point before forming a handle? Or is the whole pattern negated?*

Answered by Greg Kuhn 2000-08-05

Correct breakout moves will clear and close above their pivot points the first day. In the case of negative price reversal, if a new, tight handle develops from this point, the intraday high on the price reversal becomes the next pivot price.

Q: *In intermediate-term trading, when the right side of a cup is made by a climax run and the stock breaks out of a properly formed cup or cup-and-handle, is there a higher risk of failure? If so, can you identify which features are more consistent with failure or success? The reason I ask this is because many of the stocks breaking out have the right side formed in such a way, and it seems that they are failing.*

Answered by Greg Kuhn 2000-07-15

A climax run into the peak at the right side of the base doesn't negate the potential of the next breakout from a properly formed base. I have vast experience with what you're asking and have found no correlation of a prior climax run as an indicator of success or failure. A good example of this is the Internet stocks from 1997 through early this year. Check out all of the climax runs that Amazon.com (AMZN) had during its move from 1997 through 1999; yet it managed to break out of more sound basing patterns. Going back even further, check out NBTY during its 1992–93 run. What's going on with some of the recent breakout failures has more to do with market conditions than anything else—or even potential problems with a company's business that haven't become obvious to us yet. Don't read too much into anything that goes on in the market—there is *no* Holy Grail.

Q: *After being stopped out of four cup-and-handle setups with small losses in the last few days, I'm beginning to believe that the cup-and-handle is a higher-risk technical setup in this type of market than is buying off breakouts from double bottoms (which I think Kevin Marder calls "cheating"). You are just buying*

too high when the market could be in the midst of a bear rally. I would like your opinion on this and wonder whether you can start showing more double-bottom opportunities.

Answered by Kevin Marder 2000-07-08
I disagree with your assertion that a cup-and-handle is a higher-risk entry than buying a double-bottom base as it clears the midpoint of the "W." Anytime you're dealing with less resistance overhead, you're better off. In most cases, a cup-and-handle should offer less resistance than a double bottom, if you buy the latter just above the midpoint of the "W." Yes, there have been some cup-and-handles that have failed thus far, Nvidia being one. But I believe this to be a function of the general market, what with its unimpressive volume. Remember, a stock needs volume to ensure adequate follow-through since many players will sell when the follow-through isn't there. Did you ensure that your entries were made on stocks that had major volume on the day of their breakouts? Also, were the fundamentals—for example, the earnings growth—solid?

Q: I cannot watch the markets during the day. What strategy could I use to buy breakouts? I have been waiting for the stock to break the high of the handle and then would buy the next day. Obviously, this puts me in at a higher price. Do you have any suggestions for a strategy? Could I buy somewhere in the handle?

Answered by Kevin Marder 2000-06-10
I've never attempted to trade without being in front of a screen all day, so I'm sorry, but I can't comment on how to trade without watching the market all day. However, understand that a cup-without-handle is a higher-risk entry: If you choose to take the trade, I suggest using a stop that's tighter than your usual stop, and perhaps a position size that's smaller than your usual position size. If you "cheat" and buy a stock that's still forming a handle, be aware that you're again taking a higher-risk position. Since there are currently many stocks that are in various stages of setting up, I'd recommend being choosy about picking your spots. I hope this helps.

Q: *Are high-level cup-and-handle patterns better than big-picture cup-and-handles (e.g., TECD and TQNT as a big cup-and-handle)? Do big-picture ones fail more often than high-level ones?*

Answered by Marc Dupée 1999-06-19

Generally, high-level or "micro" cup-and-handle patterns are more reliable for short-term trades, and big-picture cup-and-handle patterns work better for longer-term trades. But more often than not, you will find that micro cups are just pauses, or pullbacks, in high-momentum stocks on their way to higher ground. Micro cups can present excellent opportunities for getting in on running markets before the next step up.

So which is better? They're both good if they have momentum behind them. And when a big-picture cup-and-handle and a high-level micro cup line up to work in unison, the movement can be explosive, as the following chart sequence for Triquint Semiconductor [TQNT] shows.

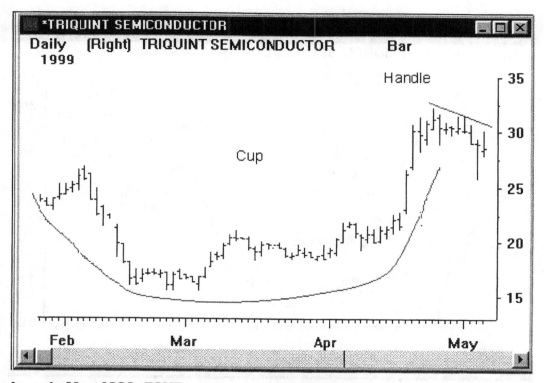

In early May 1999, TQNT sets up in a cup-and-handle pattern.
Source: Created with RealTick by Townsend Analytics, Ltd.

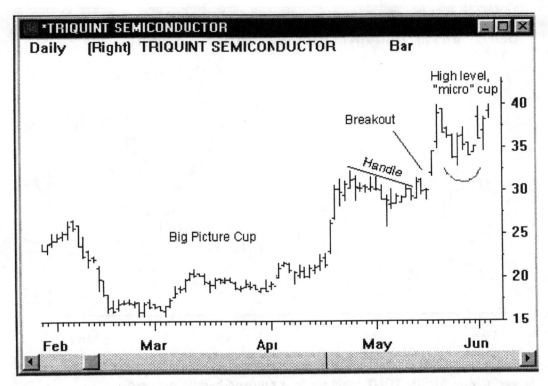

By early June, TQNT has broken out of its big-picture cup-and-handle and has formed a high-level, micro cup.
Source: Created with RealTick by Townsend Analytics, Ltd.

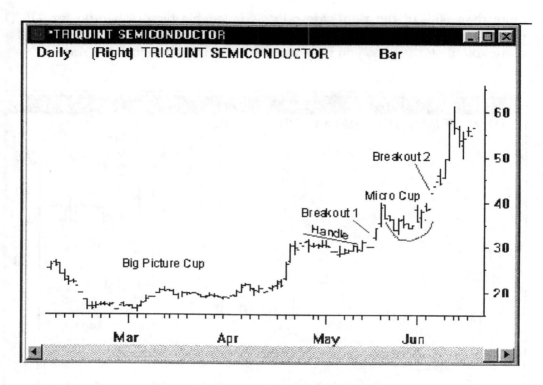

TQNT explodes almost 20 points higher after breaking out of its big-picture and high-level micro cup-and-handle patterns.
Source: Created with RealTick by Townsend Analytics, Ltd.

It is difficult to quantify the "failure" of cup-and-handles because the big-picture and micro patterns are discretionary. Tech Data (TECD), besides being in a big-picture cup-and-handle pattern, has recently failed, or traded below the bottom of its high-level micro cup. Short-term price swings occur more often than longer-term price reversals, so the logical answer is that micro-cups fail more often than big-picture cup-and-handles because they are more common.

But the important thing is identifying when a pattern has failed. The guideline we use is that a failed cup-and-handle pattern occurs if the handle retraces more than 30% of the right-side rally. A failed big-picture handle for TECD would happen below 34, which is the 30% retracement level. Since TECD is a more volatile tech stock, you may want to leave more retracement room.

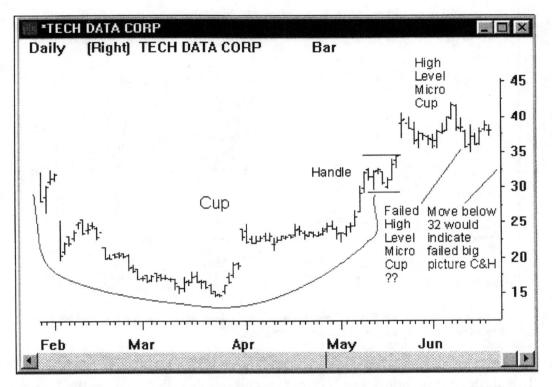

TECD's high-level micro cup fails. Failure of its big-picture pattern occurs below 32 1/2 to 34. Source: Created with RealTick by Townsend Analytics, Ltd.

Q: *Greg, as I guess you mentioned, once stocks break out from their cup handles, they sometimes tend to come back in. How far is in to be considered a failed break? The reason for the question is that I have seen this happen, and then they start up again. What is the significance of this? Is it considered a second try at the breakout, or should one just forget it?*

Answered by Greg Kuhn 2000-04-08

The first sign of failure is when a stock drops 7%–8% below its exact pivot price. In the case of a cup-and-handle breakout, the pivot price would be 1/8 point above the high of the handle. Healthy situations rarely drop this far from the pivot price—or exact breakout point—and succeed. However, if the stock is able to hang tight and re-set from that point, buy it back on the next breakout. It's not the easiest thing to do, but I try to keep my eye on a stock after being stopped out to make sure it really has failed. Then I move on to the next one.

Q: *Would you tell me when a handle is necessary after a cup-only base formation? Cups seem to form and break out rapidly, but these worry me if there's no pullback. Are there features that increase the chance of buying safely from a cup breakout that lacks a handle?*

Answered by Loren Fleckenstein 2000-05-06

A cup (sans handle) is a legitimate correction-recovery pattern. In my experience, it's more prone to failure than the cup-and-handle, but the intermediate-term trader still can trade them under the right circumstances.

The most reliable breakouts from cup-only bases tend to occur when the general market comes out of a slump and starts a new advance.

The difficult part comes in finding a buy point, since you don't have a handle to help establish a pivot point. The stock should recover up the right side of the base on strong volume with pullbacks on lighter volume. Then as the stock comes within 10%, or its pre-correction high, or closer, volume should dry up.

The volume contraction is key. It signals that existing shareholders are content to hold at the current market price. Buy as soon as the stock breaks into new high ground on a pick up in volume.

Q: *I'm a trader who, unfortunately, cannot watch during the day. My question is this: How do you determine the entry price in cup-and-handle formations? Can you then set a stop-limit buy and try to set that price (and hope if there's a pop-up opening that it comes back to cover)? Any recommendations for those of us who really set our tables before we go to bed and hope there's not too much of a mess after work would be great!*

Answered by Sterling Ten 2000-05-06

In buying the cup-and-handle setups, the entry point is generally 1/8 above the high of the handle. Preferably, this move should also be accompanied by evidence of increased volume in the stock relative to its normal activity averaged over the past 50 days, although this is not always easy to spot on an intraday basis. There's no problem with placing the stop order before you leave for work, just make sure you have a stop-loss order in once your buy order is filled. You may have to check the order status during your workday. Or if you use a live broker, you can place a contingency order with him/her, stating that once your original buy stop is executed, a stop loss order will be then placed.

Q: *If a stock breaks out of its handle first thing in the morning—at which point you're not sure whether volume is surging or not—do you take the trade, or do you wait until later in the day?*

Answered by Greg Kuhn 2000-07-22

The surest way is to extrapolate the information from the current volume. For example, if the stock breaks out within the first hour of trading, multiply the volume by 6.5 (since there are 6.5 trading hours in a day). If the extrapolated volume is about 40% above normal, you may consider the breakout as valid. A riskier way is to buy half of the position right away. If the volume is not confirmed at the end of the day, give it one more day because sometimes the volume does not come in the first day. However, you should consider selling the position on the third day if the volume did not come on the second day.

Q: *I've been a cup-and-handle trader for the past few months, and I've been fairly successful with it. But I do have a few questions about the handles: Is the peak and the high of the handle considered "Day One"? Are there a minimum number of days in which a handle should form in order for it to be valid? (I've heard three days minimum, but I'm not sure. Can you have a two-day handle?) And I do understand that "upward wedging" handles, as defined by their intraday lows, are failure prone. But I have recently observed a number of cup-and-handles forming in which the handle initially wedges down for five days or more, then wedges up for four or five days (e.g., GZTC and INTC). Is this considered a valid handle? Or is this, too, prone to failure?*

Answered by Greg Kuhn 2000-07-22

The handle count begins on the first close down. The minimum time should be at least five trading days; however, although rare, I've seen some three-day handles work. (Bear in mind, though, that I've seen far more three-day handles fail. Two days is just too short.) Proper downward wedging in a handle occurs when the intraday price trades for several days below previous lows in the handle—not necessarily in succession, but throughout the handle. If, for example, the stock pulls back into a handle over two days, then spends the next six days in the handle making higher intraday highs and higher intraday lows, there would be upward wedging. I hope this explanation helps. However, it really is up to you to study this stuff over and over again, in order to get it totally ingrained in your mind.

Q: *Many stocks don't seem to make good pivot points within cup-and-handles or else they flip through them at lightning speed. Do you set stop-buy orders and check when you can later in the day? What happens when the price passes through the pivot but not at 50% or more of its average volume, then volume picks up later, but the price is beyond 5% from the pivot?*

Answered by Kevin Marder 2000-03-11

For the benefit of our readership, let's review what pivot points are. When it comes to cup-and-handles, traders set their pivot points at the line of least resistance. In a cup-and-handle, the pivot point is 1/8 above the peak price in the handle. At this point the stock faces little or no resistance to the upside. However, the upward move must be accompanied by at least a 50% increase of the average volume.

Increased volume shows institutional interest in the stock. The price action can move very quickly if there is heavy institutional buying for that stock. Thus, most traders will place stop-buy orders 1/8 above the peak price in the handle. Remember that you do not have to wait for the volume to achieve a 50% increase or more. You will get a good idea of whether the volume will reach the desirable level if, for example, it is two hours into the trading day and the volume for your stock is 400,000 shares, and the average volume is 500,000. Four hundred thousand is 80% of 500,000 and the market will be open for another 5 1/2 hours. At such a rate (200,000 shares per hour), your stock will be trading at over 1.2 million shares by the time the market closes—and that is more than 50% over the average volume of 500,000. However, be careful of chasing stocks that are 5% or more above your buying pivot point.

Although it can be frustrating to see a setup take off and leave you behind, stick to your trading rules and preserve your trading capital.

Q: *I know the ideal volume configuration during the handle is a volume dry-up, especially along the price lows. My question is how do you interpret a high-volume handle that has all of the other proper characteristics? Is this a situation that is faulty like a wedging handle?*

Answered by Greg Kuhn 2000-08-19
In addition to volume dry-up in the handle, tight day-to-day price variations in the handle are just as important. If the high volume occurs on up days alongside nice, tight price areas on the other days, this would be fine. However, if all you see are several big up days on high volume, which will look too erratic and loose, then it's probably not the handle. There should be several days in the handle where there's little price change day-to-day.

GILLIGAN'S ISLAND REVERSAL

Q: *Jeff, what is a Gilligan Reversal? Where would I find an explanation? And do I want one or not? If I am reading your articles correctly, IONA just pulled one on Friday. And it did almost the same thing two weeks ago, edging ever higher afterward. My current assumption is that the reversal forms the initial days of a pennant formation. I think I'm looking at good things, especially given your article where you mentioned IDTI and AMCC doing this. But SCMR went the wrong way, so it could be that a Gilligan reversal offers no bias, but is simply a kind of setup.*

Answered by Jeff Cooper 2000-09-09
Gilligan's Island setups **can** form the beginnings of pennants. Sometimes they do and sometimes not. They do not offer any longer-term bias. For me, they are simply a short-term setup I utilize as a momentum trader. The rules for buy setups are: First, the stock must gap open down to a new two-month low. Second, it must close at or in the top 50% of its daily range and equal to or above its opening price. You will enter the following day one tick above the previous day's high. For sells, the rules are reversed.

HEAD AND SHOULDERS

Q: *What should I do when the indices are forming head-and-shoulder top patterns but my individual stocks are forming cup-and-handle patterns? Meaning, when the index is saying, "get the heck out," but my individual stocks are saying, "get in," which should I listen to?*

Answered by Mark Etzkorn 1999-10-09
Good question, but one for which there is no definitive answer. From a purely technical viewpoint, many traders might say the only thing that matters is the signal in the particular stock you're watching. However, trading in that kind of analysis "vacuum" is not advisable. It is always a good idea to take into consideration the strength (or weakness) of the overall market as well as the strength (or weakness) of the sector to which your stock belongs before taking a long (or short) position.

Sector indexes and broader market indexes are valuable tools; if they suggest the market is going down when your stock says it wants to go up, you should ask yourself why. Obviously, there are any number of legitimate reasons—earnings announcements, takeover news, and so on—that may cause a particular stock to diverge from its sector and the overall market, and you must take these into consideration.

Regarding the current situation, consider a couple of things: First, from a technical standpoint, the head-and-shoulders (H&S) top pattern in the popular stock indexes is indeed a warning that a reversal or substantial correction by the overall market is possible.

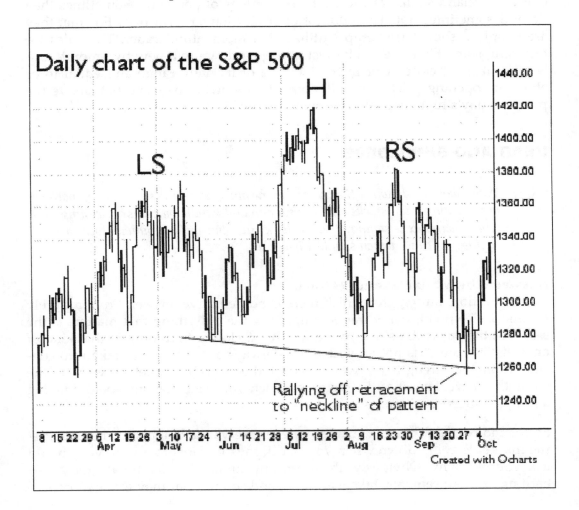

Second, the chart above makes it clear the H&S pattern in the S&P 500 has not, as of Oct. 6, 1999, penetrated the "neckline" of the pattern, i.e., the support level implied by connecting the relative lows between the head and the two shoulders. In other words, the pattern has not triggered a sell signal. In fact, the market has staged a nice rally off this low and is threatening to negate the pattern with a move, first, above the right shoulder, and second, with a solid move above the head (which would constitute a major upside breakout). But this has not occurred yet, either.

In short: The overall market is in limbo. It has bounced off support but has not yet pushed far enough to the upside to clearly indicate another major leg of the bull market is underway. If you subscribe to the theory of using the action in one of the major indexes as a filter—trading on the long side only when an index is "long," and selling only when it is "short" (and there is some validity to this basic approach), your question answers itself.

But let's dig a little deeper. One thing you don't address is the time frame of the particular market you're looking at. The H&S pattern on the daily chart represents a longer-term potential top. What magnitude time frame are you talking about for your trade? If the cup-and-handle pattern you're watching is on a 15-minute chart, it is obviously less significant than the major H&S developing on the daily chart.

So where does that leave you on a practical basis? If you do take a trade, you might consider the following risk-control measures:

1. **Establishing a smaller position, using tighter stops, or both.**

2. **Hedging the trade with an option position.**

3. **Using a filter to make your trade entry criteria more stringent.**
   Examples:

   a. Waiting for a stronger signal (say, three or four up closes in a row before going long when you normally might only wait for consecutive up closes)

   b. Waiting for a confirming signal from another system or strategy

c. Waiting for the sector index to turn bullish, or some combination of these

d. You also might, as mentioned before, consult the performance of other key stocks in the sector. This way, you're entering only when the market is showing strong upside momentum. Obviously, such techniques will mean you'll miss part of the move, but that is the price you pay for such insurance.

Using a pattern failure is actually an interesting kind of approach. Wait for the index to trigger a bullish setup (in this case, make a solid move to the upside, negating the bearish head-and-shoulders pattern). A higher-risk condition for this would be a move above the high of the right shoulder, while a lower-risk condition would be a move above the head.

But consider one last point: The fact that taking the trade requires a number of special criteria (that is, if you believe the arguments outlined here make sense) to be in place suggests the trade you are considering is relatively high risk. When one factor—and it must be an important one, or you wouldn't have brought it up—is so obviously not in your favor, you need to ask yourself if such a trade is worth the risk, and if you have a solid plan to control that risk. Why not wait until all the signals are in your favor before taking a trade? Yes, it's true you have to be able to pull the trigger on a trade, but if you're going to be wrong, it's better to be wrong and not lose money. There will always be other trade opportunities

HOOK TO THE UPSIDE

Q: *On Aug. 12, Jeff Cooper stated, "Legato (LGTO) may be a failed hook to the upside. If it breaks, it could break big." What does "a failed hook to the upside" mean? Does he think it is going to break up or down?*

Answered by Marc Dupée 1999-08-21
A "hook to the upside" occurs when a stock pulls back from a high, and then resumes its uptrend. To identify a hook, look for a stock to violate the pullback's (down) trendline and to break out above the previous day's high.

On 8/12/99, Legato (LGTO) gapped open above the previous two days' highs and broke above the pullback trendline (A). However, the same morning, LGTO traded back below the trendline and the highs of the past two days, casting doubt on the soundness of the breakout (B on the chart). A "failed hook to the upside" means the stock would have broken DOWN. The situation did not develop. Legato recovered and rallied. Jeff was giving a real-time heads up in that commentary about a potentially implosive situation: "If it breaks (down), it could break big." Jeff later commented on the situation, "It's not the break of a trendline that counts; it's the movement thereafter; you've got to watch the flush-out." A stock should move strongly in the direction of a breakout to be valid, but often the strong move in the direction of the underlying trend will occur the second time through after the stock dips back to flush out any weak hands.

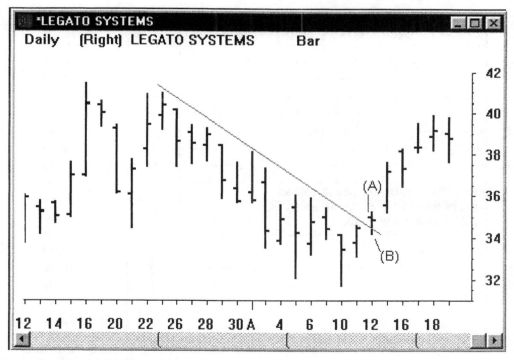

Source: Created with RealTick III by Townsend Analytics.

HOT IPO

Q: *I am confused by your term Hot IPO. You defined it as trading at least 15% higher within the first five trading days after going public and then a pull back for two to four days. Do you mean 15% from the offering price or where it opens? And when can the pullback occur? Two days later, two weeks or two months later? Would NTRO be an example of a Hot IPO? What about Silverstream (SSSW)?*

Answered by Jeff Cooper 1999-08-28

A Hot IPO trades up at least 15% from its offering price. The pullback would be its first pullback from highs, whether days or weeks later. Yes, NTRO is a good example. SSSW also is a Hot IPO pullback, as it was priced at 16, opened at 32 and pulled back to 24.

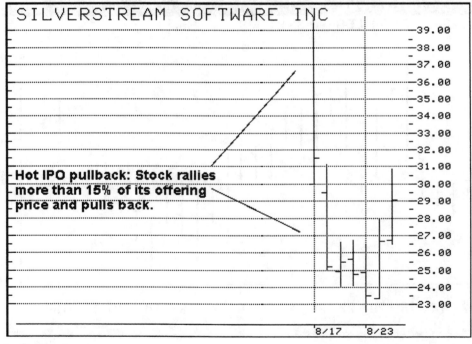

Source: Quote.com.

LIZARD TAILS

Q: *What are the "tails" that Jeff Cooper talks about and how do you trade them?*

Answered by Marc Dupée 1999-05-01

Tails, or more specifically "Lizard Tails," are reversal setups that Jeff Cooper first made public in his book *Hit and Run Trading*. For buy setups, the tail is formed on a bar chart when the opening and closing prices are in the top 25% of the daily range and the low of the day stretches down to make a new 10-day low. For short-sale setups, the open and close are in the bottom 25% of the daily range and the high of the day, the tail, is a 10-day high.

To trade them, buy 1/8 above the high of the Lizard Tail buy setup day, and sell 1/8 below the low of the Lizard Tail sell setup day. Place your protective stops 1 point from your buy or sell orders and exit before the day's close. This pattern is a one-day trade.

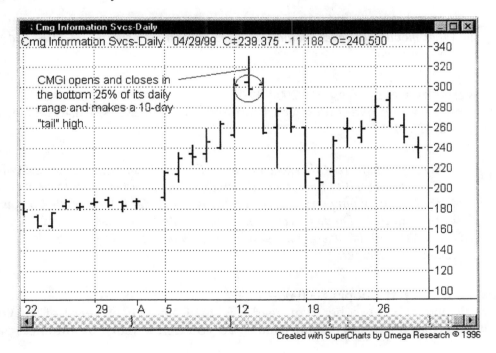

MOVING AVERAGES

Q: *Kevin Haggerty, in your lesson on 1-2-3 reversal patterns, your examples point out the various percentages of the prices above the 50-day and 200-day EMAs. Also, you note the percentages of the several corrections. What is the significance of these percentages? I understand the interest in the Fibonacci percentages, but not the others.*

Answered by Kevin Haggerty 2000-12-23
I use both Fibonacci point and percent RT numbers. I am also aware of extended percent levels above the moving averages. Each stock or index has certain tendencies, and when they reach those extended levels, you must be aware of reversal patterns. Very often you will see a negative or positive divergence in RSI and stochastics at these extreme levels, and that is what alerts you to a trade.

Q: *What moving averages should I apply to my intraday charts (60-, 10-, and five-minutes)?*

Answered by Kevin Haggerty 2000-04-15
I generally use the five-minute chart intraday. For the EMAs, I use the 20-, 60- and 260-EMA.

Q: *Hello, Jeff. I have read that when a stock climbs substantially above its 20-day moving average, it is time to sell the stock, for it has a tendency to snap back to its 20-day moving average when it becomes extended. First of all, do you agree with that? Do you recommend shorting stocks that have moved high above their 20-day averages, and how high above the 20-day average is extended on average?*

Answered by Jeff Cooper 2000-08-26
I would like to know where you read this, for I have never heard of it. When you state that a stock is extended, how do you define that—by time, percent-

age above the 20-day MA, or points? Different conditions are present in every stock's movement and mean different things to different traders. There is no blanket answer to how far a stock can get above the 20-day moving average before it is "too far." In answer to the second part of your question, the answer is no, I do not recommend shorting stocks simply because they have risen over their 20-day moving average. Many times, stocks are met with buying when they pull back to their 20-day MA in a method traders have named the "Holy Grail." But buying a stock pulling back in this manner and shorting are two different things entirely. What you must do is learn the behavior of the stock and how it acts around an indicator like a moving average, not arbitrarily trade a stock, based on a blanket set of rules.

Q: *I have been watching and playing CTXS for the past few weeks. It has been rising, and as of today, it is less than 2% under its 50-day EMA. I have been waiting for it to crack the 50-day EMA before buying in. Is this a good strategy?*

Answered by Eddie Kwong 2000-09-02
As you may be aware, we cannot give any recommendations on specific stocks. So I will speak to the general issue of using moving averages in your analysis. In my own experience, widely followed moving averages such as the 50- and 200-day are useful, but only under certain circumstances. For one thing, I would only pay attention to a stock's moving average if there were some recent history of support or resistance coming in off the moving average. In other words, you see bounces or marked pauses in the price action at the moving average. This kind of action suggests that there's a school of fish following the moving average, and they're all acting in unison. Secondly, and most importantly, I would never ever trade off a moving average breakout or bounce alone. You need to look at many other factors, such as the prevailing trends of a stock, price patterns, volume and retracements. For me to take a trade, I'd want to see multiple alerts coming at a certain price.

Q: *Should a daytrader take into consideration the 200-, 50-, and 10-day moving averages when timing the purchase and sale of a stock? If so, what are a few good techniques with regards to these averages that a trader should use as part of his trading system?*

Answered by Marc Dupée 1999-05-01

Moving averages (MAs) are among the most commonly used tools to make trading decisions. You should consider the 200-, 50- and 10-day moving averages, but for different reasons. Traditionally, a short-term average like a 10-day moving average is used for timing the entry of a trade when it crosses a slower, 20- or 50-day moving average.

For instance, when the faster (10-day) average crosses above the slower (20- or 50-day MA) a buy signal is generated, especially when both averages point up, a setup known as a golden cross.

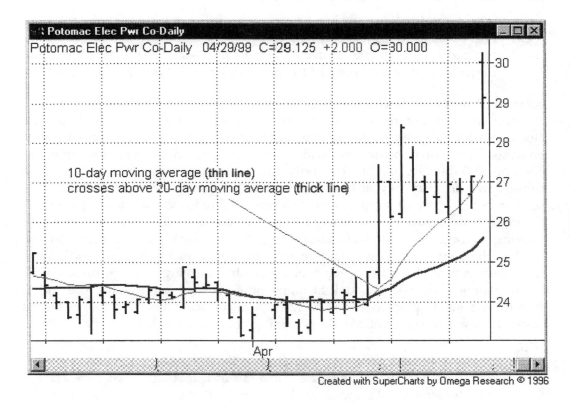

The opposite action generates a sell signal. For daytrading, the same rules apply when using the 200-, 50- or 10-period moving averages. You just change the time frame to 60-, 15-, or 10-minute (or some other time period) bars.

Moving averages smooth price fluctuations, which make them useful for defining trends. The longer (50- to 200-day) moving averages often contain the price action in a trending market, acting as support in bull markets and resistance in bear markets. Breakdowns below the 50-day moving average sometimes indicate an up trend has reversed and moves below the 200-day average often serve as confirmation that a bearish trend is in place.

Of course, markets often penetrate moving averages only to reverse and resume their previous trends. As a result, most traders who use moving averages use some kind of filtering system to confirm signals. For example, they might require a certain number of closes above the moving average before considering it a valid buy signal, or require the market to penetrate the moving average by a certain amount.

At TradingMarkets.com we keep a close eye on the 50-day exponential moving average (EMA), which uses a logarithm that emphasizes recent price action over past price movement. (The EMA essentially is a special form of "weighted" moving average; the "simple," or arithmetic moving average does not weight prices.) Because institutions closely track the 50-day EMA to make trading decisions, we watch it, too, using it as a low-risk inflection point to re-enter markets that have been performing well.

For instance, Kevin Haggerty mentioned in his commentary last week how the S&P 500 Index and several individual stocks had set up at their 50-day EMAs. After trading down to its 50-day EMA, the S&P cash closed in the top 25% of its daily range on 4/20/99. A "buy signal" would have been triggered on a move above the high of that bar (1306.25), with a protective stop below the low of that bar.

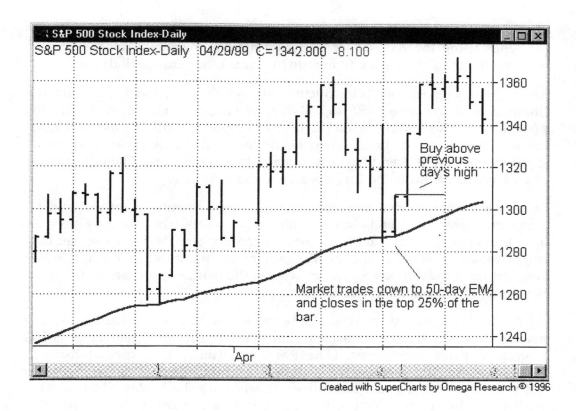

S&P 500 Stock Index-Daily

S&P 500 Stock Index-Daily 04/29/99 C=1342.800 -8.100

Buy above
previous
day's high

Market trades down to 50-day EMA
and closes in the top 25% of the
bar.

Created with SuperCharts by Omega Research © 1996

Here are similar examples (on the same date) in individual stocks.

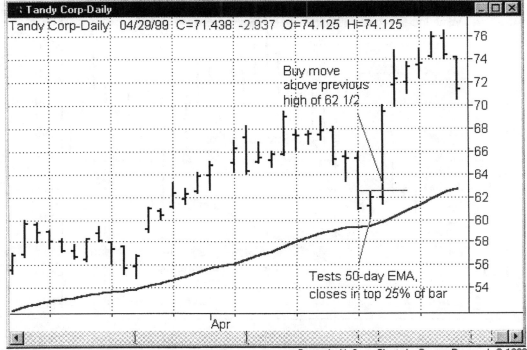

Chart annotations:
- Tandy Corp-Daily: 04/29/99 C=71.438 -2.937 O=74.125 H=74.125
- Buy move above previous high of 62 1/2
- Tests 50-day EMA, closes in top 25% of bar
- Apr
- Created with SuperCharts by Omega Research ® 1996

America Online Inc-Daily

America Online Inc-Daily   04/29/99   C=141.375   -1.625   O=140.500

Buy above high
of bar

AOL tests the 50-day EMA and
then closes in the top 25% of the bar.

Created with SuperCharts by Omega Research ® 1996

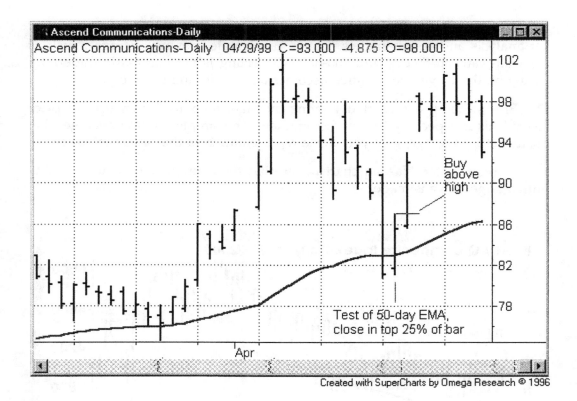

Ascend Communications-Daily

Ascend Communications-Daily 04/29/99 C=93.000 -4.875 O=98.000

Buy above high

Test of 50-day EMA, close in top 25% of bar

Apr

Created with SuperCharts by Omega Research © 1996

Q: *I noticed that the 200-day moving average referenced on your chart is actually the 200-day simple moving average, whereas others, such as Kevin Haggerty, seem to prefer exponential moving averages. Is that just a matter of personal preference or has your work shown one to be more effective than the other? I noticed that the low of the Tuesday meltdown touched the 200-EMA almost right to the penny. Apparently someone was watching that level pretty closely (it also coincided with approximately the .618 retracement of the move from the October low to the March high).*

Answered by Dave Landry 2000-04-15
In my own personal trading and analysis I often use exponential moving aver-

ages. This is especially true in the futures markets. However, in my stock market analysis and commentaries, I often use simple moving averages, such as the well-watched 50-day and 200-day. My feeling is with so many traders focusing on these averages, it often becomes a self-fulfilling prophecy.

The EMAs, being a weighted moving average, tend to "catch up" to price faster. This is especially true in fast markets. The simple moving averages, being an actual average, give you a true representation of the "average" price.

You'll notice in the Nasdaq chart below that the averages often run together until a large move is made.

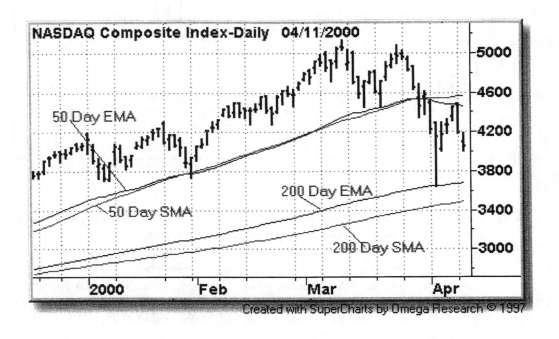

It really becomes a matter of personal preference. I like to have all tools at my disposal. Therefore, I'll often mix it up a bit, using simple for short-term periods (say 10 days or less) and EMAs for longer-term periods (say 20 days or more).

By the way, nice observation on the Nasdaq nailing the 200-day EMA and .618.

OPENING REVERSAL

Q: *What does it mean to fade?*

Answered by Kevin Haggerty 2000-07-15
To fade means to sell into a rally and to buy into a decline. You are trading like the specialists and market makers. Volatility, which is an overreaction to news, etc., will usually revert to the mean.

Q: *I like your opening reversal trade. Can you tell me: 1) What stocks make the best opening reversal candidates? 2) I am using three-minute bar charts, but I find the reversals trade through their opening price quickly and I miss the majority of the move. Should I anticipate the trade and trade before it trades through? Should I switch to one- or two-minute data? 3) Any other related info on reversals and flip tops would be appreciated. 4) One last thing: I use one 17" monitor. What's the best way to watch for reversals, and what's the max # of stocks I should be watching for in these early moves?*

Answered by Kevin Haggerty 2000-02-12
In answer to your questions: 1) The ones that are down due to S&P futures action (reverse for sells), but are acting better than market. 2) No, the stock must trade below the opening by more than, say, 1/8 or 1/4. There is too much erratic movement right at the opening. You are looking for the first countertrend to the opening move. 3) They will usually be the stocks that acted best the day before. 4) It is easiest when you have your quote page set up as follows: OPEN/LAST/HIGH/LOW. That will enable you to pick up reversals quickly. Start with your core list, but be ready to jump on best-relative-performing stocks that day.

Q: *Thank you so much, Kevin Haggerty, for your commentary on fading emotional openings (March 14). I see this opportunity very often when a stock gaps up on the open, it will usually fall back to fill the gap and more. My problem is pulling the trigger. I see the stocks bidding up pre-market and I fear that they will continue going up, so I don't short. Then they proceed to fall and I've missed another great trade. My question is, what signal do you use when shorting an "emotional" opening? Should I just short the opening and hope the stock falls back?*

Answered by Kevin Haggerty 2000-04-01
On listed stocks, I watch the pre-opening indications on stocks that are going to open more than normal and if I think it's overdone, I will enter at market on the open. For OTC stocks, I will look for a reversal bar on my five- or three-minute charts and some follow through to confirm and take position. For example, if I am looking to go long, I want to see a stock trading at the mid-point between the bid and the ask, and for a stock to trade above the high of the prior bar, which should have been a low, and the close was below the opening. That is just a quick price reversal. I also want to see the NYSE ticks improving and some other stocks or sectors turning green. Good luck in your trading. You must be careful on your stock selection—no fraud or accounting problems. I look for futures-related and earnings-related trades that get overdone on gaps.

OUTSIDE DAYS

Q: *What is an "outside" day? What are the parameters for buying or not buying on an "outside" day? How does that contrast with an "inside" day?*

Answered by Sterling Ten 2000-08-26
An "outside" day means the trading range for today is wider than the previous trading day. When you look at the daily chart, you should see today's high is higher than yesterday's high and today's low is lower than yesterday's low. Outside days usually indicate expansion in volatility or possible change

in direction, depending on where the stock closed. For instance, if a stock is in an uptrend and forms an outside day, but closes strongly in the top 25% of to-day's range, it usually means that weak hands were shaken out and fresh buy-ers came in to move the stock back up. Most of time, this means that the stock has a chance to continue the upward movement. On the other hand, if the stock closed within the bottom 25% of the day's range, it may indicate a trend reversal to the downside.

An "inside" day is the opposite of the outside day, which means that today's high is lower than the previous day's high and today's low is higher than yes-terday's low. An inside day indicates volatility contraction. When a stock forms a series of inside days (in the form of a triangle), it shows indecision in the trend. The stock can move higher if it takes out the recent high or it can move lower if the stock breaks below the bottom of the triangle.

Q: *What is the significance of outside days?*

Answered by Marc Dupée 1999-05-22
Outside days can mean many things—from strong conviction to uncertainty and doubt. An outside day's meaning depends on where in a chart's pattern it occurs and where it closes.

One of the best practical applications of outside days is Jeff Cooper's "Rever-sal New Highs Method." It is actually a continuation pattern and not a "trend" reversal. The reversal (for buys) refers to a stock selling off intraday to trade under the previous day's low, then reversing to shoot to new highs, forming an outside day. It is somewhat rare, but had you known about it this week, you might have been able to take part in a 7-point move in Hewlett-Packard.

Let's review the setup. A stock must trade below yesterday's low, then trade above yesterday's high, forming an outside day. Also, the stock must hit a new 60-day high and the outside day's range must be the largest of the past five days. Buy 1/16 above the outside day's high and risk 1 point (sells are re-versed).

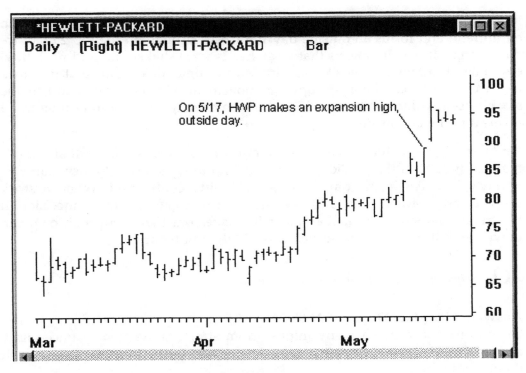

*HEWLETT-PACKARD

Daily   [Right] HEWLETT-PACKARD   Bar

On 5/17, HWP makes an expansion high, outside day.

100
95
90
85
80
75
70
65
60

Mar   Apr   May

Source: Created with RealTick by Townsend Analytics, Ltd.

SLIM JIMS

Q: *Can someone give me an explanation and/or a chart as to what a Slim Jim pattern is?*

Answered by Marc Dupée 2000-06-03
A Slim Jim is a narrow-range intraday consolidation pattern that forms at or near the high or low of the day. Generally speaking, the longer and tighter the consolidation, the more explosive the eventual breakout. This pattern is described in greater detail in *TradingMarkets.com Guide to Conquering the Trading Markets.*

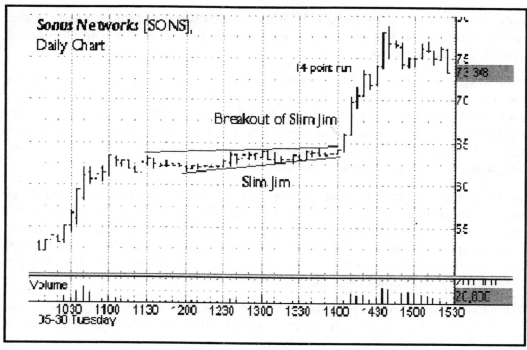

Source: Qcharts.

Q: *You gave an example of a pattern called a "Slim Jim" and used Hewlett-Packard for the example. I have two questions regarding this pattern. 1) Can this pattern be used in the futures markets? 2) This pattern appears to me to look very much like "Spike & Ledge" which is detailed in* Street Smarts, *with the exception that "SJ" trades in the direction of the price thrust and the "S&L" trades against the price thrust. If this is so, is there a way to determine which pattern is most likely to manifest itself after the price thrust and during the consolidation phase?*

Answered by Marc Dupée 1999-06-11
Slim Jims are narrow-range, intraday continuation patterns that form at, or near, the high or low of the day. They present a low-risk method of entering a stock just before "the elephants" get on board. Kevin Haggerty designed the

pattern to take advantage of accelerating momentum generated by institutions, hedge funds, specialists and retail investors as they dog-pile into closely followed, big-name stocks.

Technically, in order to take advantage of the institutional piling-on effect, you can only trade Slim Jims in the most widely followed S&P and Dow stocks, and not in the futures markets. But high-level consolidations remain a valid continuation pattern in any market, although you will not find the same institutional dynamics at work. But similar patterns exist, and we'll look at an example soon. First, let's review the Slim Jim.

A Slim Jim buy signal occurs on a five-minute bar chart when a market consolidates in a tight range (at least 8–10 bars) at or near the high of the day (sells are reversed). Ideally, the stock is a large-cap S&P stock, trading above its 50- and 200-day moving average. For longs, price and volume should be increasing on the time-and-sales screen. Buy on the first breakout above the Slim Jim consolidation and risk 1/4 point.

Let's look at a recent example of a Slim Jim in a Dow component stock, Caterpillar (CAT). You may also want to review the example presented in the 5/22/99 archive.

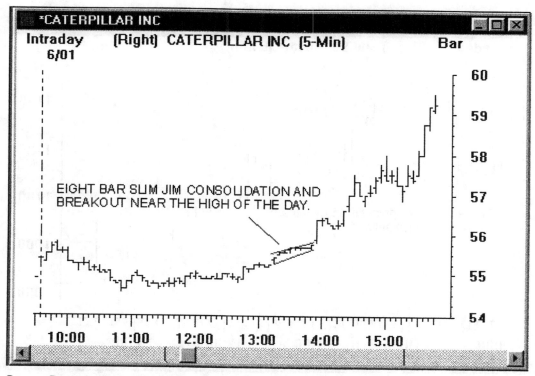

Source: Created with RealTick by Townsend Analytics, Ltd.

The "Spike and Ledge" indeed shares characteristics with the SJ, but as you point out, it is an intraday reversal, rather than continuation pattern. The Spike and Ledge, from Connors' and Raschke's *Street Smarts*, sets up after a big spike, or parabolic move (up or down), in a move typical of exhaustion patterns. This differentiates it from the Slim Jim: A Slim Jim consolidates near a high, and then continues or spikes higher.

Let's review the Spike-and-Ledge setup by looking at two back-to-back examples this week in Cocoa.

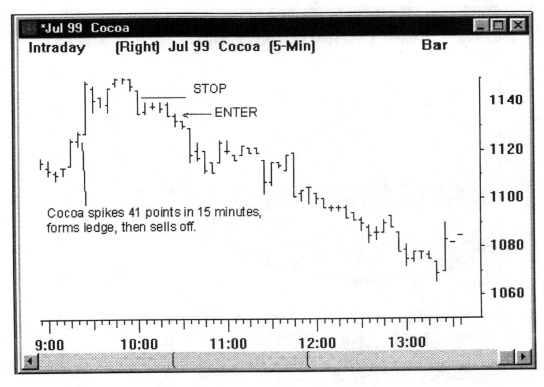

Source: RealTick by Townsend Analytics, Ltd.

A Spike-and-Ledge occurred again the following day in cocoa:

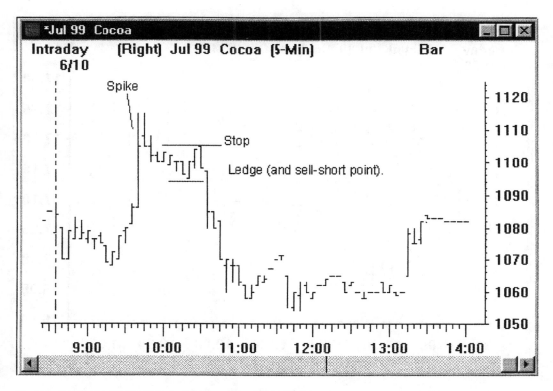

Source: Created with RealTick by Townsend Analytics, Ltd.

Slim Jim-like patterns exist in futures, and they are useful patterns for identifying low-risk, high-potential trades. A Slim Jim-like trade set up in bean oil on Thursday.

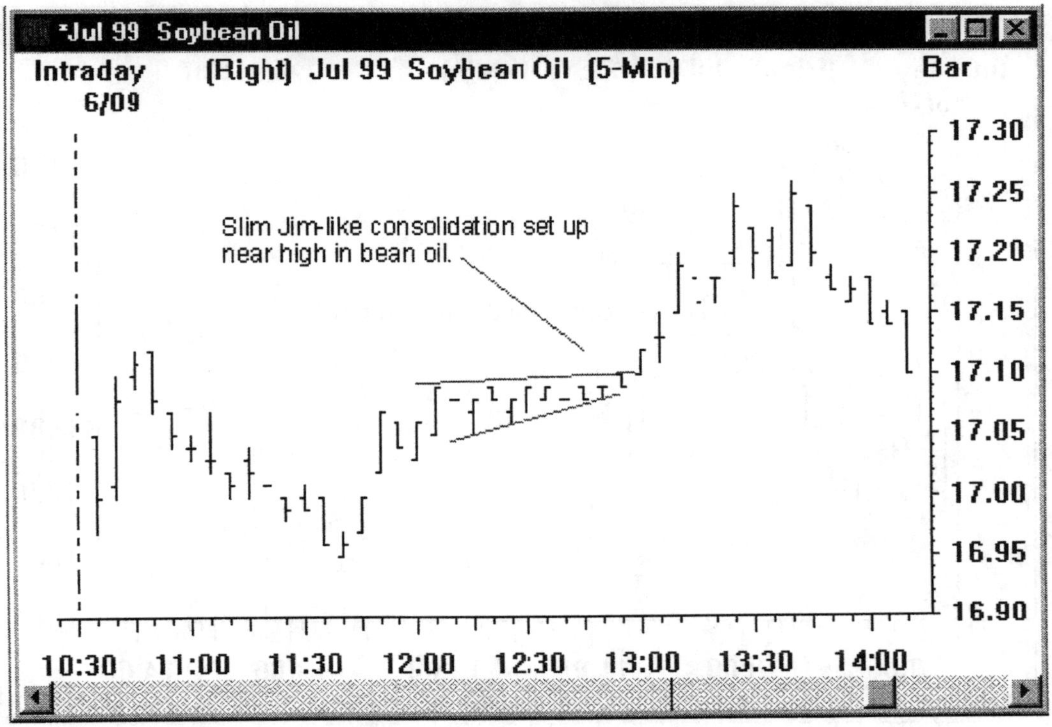

*Jul 99 Soybean Oil
Intraday 6/09
[Right] Jul 99 Soybean Oil [5-Min]
Bar
Slim Jim-like consolidation set up near high in bean oil.
17.30
17.25
17.20
17.15
17.10
17.05
17.00
16.95
16.90
10:30
11:00
11:30
12:00
12:30
13:00
13:30
14:00

Source: Created with RealTick by Townsend Analytics, Ltd.

Q: *I recently saw the Slim Jim in Kevin Haggerty's daytrading course. This has been my bread-and-butter trading approach for a long time, although my parameters are more loosely defined. This strategy alone, when properly traded, can make one a consistent, extremely profitable trader. My question is regarding your exit strategy. The reason I ask is that I have found the real power behind this approach to be the exit. I also risk 1/2 to 1 point depending on the price of the stock and the current Level II dynamics. But I don't use a trailing stop. I have done a lot of research into how far price will go off of these setups. I have found that stock prices dictate this. For example, for $50–$75 stocks, a $4 move is an extremely high probability if the setup is valid with slight ad-*

justments for the volatility of the stock. I won't risk more, but I won't start selling until the stock starts nearing my profit targets. This exit strategy gives me extremely favorably risk/reward and a high number of winning trades. It's the daytrader's dream. I was wondering about your thoughts and experience with this type of exit as well as what time charts you are keying off of. I personally have found five-minute charts give the best setups.

Answered by Kevin Haggerty 2000-12-30
I don't use absolute profit targets. I let the market and stock dynamics take me out. You sound like you are managing your trades well, but if you have to make choice on exit, go with the market, not the profit target. It sounds to me like you are doing that. I also love to trade the failure and go as it breaks out above pattern high the second time. You absolutely can be very profitable just trading Slim Jims and its sister consolidations, but you would be amazed at how many traders just refuse to go with something that appears simple. They are always looking for complex strategies and Holy Grail daytrading systems, but there are none.

SUPPORT AND RESISTANCE

Q: *Is there any easy way to predict resistance or support level of a stock?*

Answered by Mark Etzkorn 1999-07-17
Yes, there is, but it's not foolproof. A good place to look for support or resistance is at levels of former support and resistance, or other significant price patterns—major tops and bottoms, relative swing highs and lows, etc.

One of the basic tenets of support and resistance is that former support becomes future resistance and former resistance becomes future support. Here is a good example of this on a weekly chart of the S&P futures; it also highlights some important aspects of support and resistance.

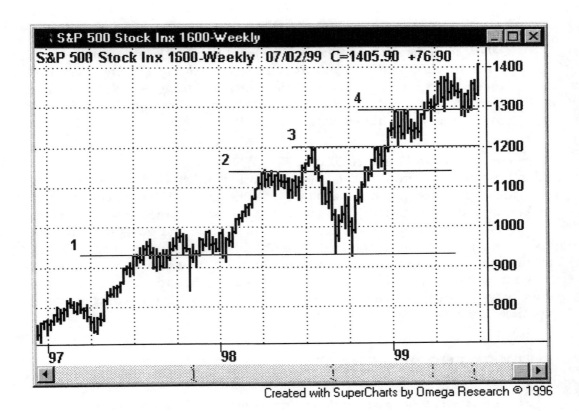

S&P 500 Stock Inx 1600-Weekly

S&P 500 Stock Inx 1600-Weekly 07/02/99 C=1405.90 +76.90

Created with SuperCharts by Omega Research © 1996

First, notice that almost all the support (and some of the resistance) levels over this two-and-a-half year period can be traced back to previous support, resistance or relative high points (see lines 1–4).

Next, notice that support and resistance are almost never precise price levels, but rather, price ranges. The dramatic correction in fall 1998 dropped to around the middle of the fall 1997 consolidation (line 1); the top of the early 1999 trading range provided relatively accurate support for the spring selloff (line 4). The top in the summer of 1998 (line 3), however, proved to be a very precise resistance level toward the end of that year, and subsequently, a support level in early 1999.

But keep in mind there is no law requiring stocks or futures to correct or turn around at such obvious levels. You must protect yourself with stops if you plan to take trades at such points.

Fibonacci

Q: *I am looking for a short-but-sweet explanation of Fibonacci numbers and a good setting for them based on daytrading.*

Answered by Tsutae Kamada 2000-11-04

Fibonacci numbers are used to calculate potential pivot points or turning points of the stock. The most important numbers to remember are 38.2%, 50%, and 61.8%. For example, on Nov. 1, Yahoo hit its intraday high of 64 at 1:00 P.M. (EST) and began to decline. Its intraday low of 57 was recorded at 9:30 A.M. How far would Yahoo go down before the bounce? We can possibly answer this question by utilizing Fibonacci numbers. First, we subtract the intraday low from the intraday high (64 − 57 = 7). Then we will multiply this number by 38.2% (7 × 0.382 = 2.674). Now subtract this number from the intraday high to get a potential pivot point (64 − 2.674 = 61.326). Amazingly, Yahoo hit 61 3/8 (61.375) at 1:10 P.M. and began to bounce. At 1:55 P.M., Yahoo reached its intraday high of 67. Keep in mind that Fibonacci numbers (like every other technical tool you're likely to run across) are not the Holy Grail. It doesn't always work. You should only take a trade if a potential Fibonacci support or resistance level is confirmed by the developing price and volume action.

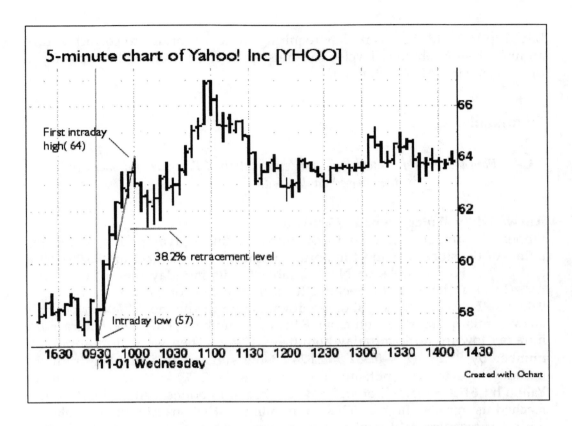

5-minute chart of Yahoo! Inc [YHOO]

First intraday high(64)

38.2% retracement level

Intraday low (57)

1630 0930 1000 1030 1100 1130 1200 1230 1300 1330 1400 1430
11-01 Wednesday

Created with Ochart

Q: *Please explain the relationship between Fibonacci numbers and the apparent tendency of some stocks to reverse direction as they approach these numbers. Fibonacci numbers/ratios exist in nature and ancient architecture—in everything from the reproduction of rabbits to the pyramids.*

Answered by David Landry 2000-01-15

The topic of Fibonacci numbers is subject to debate (often lively!) when it comes to the markets. Some believe that retracement to the Fib ratios (most commonly used are .382, .50 and .618) often provides a pivot point. Whether you believe in them or not, you can't ignore the fact that they are watched by some traders. That, in and of itself, may be reason enough to consider these ratios—in other words it could be a self-fulfilling prophecy. This may be what you have observed.

Q: *Mr. Haggerty, your knowledge of institutional trading and the patterns involved has been very useful to me and to a lot of others as well. I am interested in your use of retracement levels. Specifically, you mention the .5 RT and the .618 RT. I have spent some time working with this and just wanted to know more about it. Are there other significant retracement levels?*

Answered by Kevin Haggerty 2000-09-30
I mostly use .38, .50, .618, .786, and then some extensions of those numbers. I think Fibonacci is excellent when used with converging stock patterns and moving averages.

Q: *In one of your interviews, trader Jim Hyerczyk stated that he waited for a 50% retracement from a breakout high and the low of the trading range. If the price falls back into the trading range, he stills takes the trade? Isn't that a false breakout if it slides back? Does he miss a lot of moves waiting for the 50%? Am I missing something?*

Answered by Jim Hyerczyk 2000-01-22
The move is very similar to what Jeff Cooper looks for when he looks for pullbacks from new highs. In his system, he waits for ADX and the fast stochastic to line up properly. In my analysis, I wait for a 50% pullback combined with an uptrending Gann angle, since the strongest point on the chart is where the Gann Angle crosses the 50% price. Now, a little about techniques.

In the Jeff Cooper models, he takes the trade when the oscillator setup is identified and places, in most cases, a $2.00 stop. This is a money-management stop.

In my technique, I wait for Price and Time to set up, and my stop is placed in relationship with the Gann Angle/50% Retracement setup. Through testing, one can optimize how much a market has to break through a 50% price or Gann angle before failing.

The reason I like the setup of the two prices is because sometimes if a trader places the stop under the 50% price alone, it will be right on the Gann Angle. And in other cases, buying off of the Gann Angle alone may force the stop on the 50% price. Waiting for both to cross tries to eliminate this problem. As far as missing trades is concerned:

> Yes, trades are missed using this analysis because sometimes a market doesn't pull back 50% or reach the Gann angle. Like any system, however, you have to have rules. Buying slightly above the 50% point in anticipation of a market turn means the stop that is placed in relation to the 50% point will be greater. One more thing—Gann analysis is tougher today because of the number of contracts available to trade and the inability to computerize everything.

In principle, Jeff Cooper's technique is very close to what I do. I find his techniques fascinating.

I strongly urge you to study the Jeff Cooper material. I am not pinned to the 50% retracement. The 33%, .618 and 67% retracements combined with uptrending Gann angles can be used for buys also. The basic trading methodology of Gann was swing trading. To put it simply, he said to buy new highs and sell new lows. Like any swing system, the market does sometimes pull back following a breakout to new highs. However, the general rule is that a pullback is acceptable as long as the main bottom is not broken. Using this method can sometimes produce whipsaw trading and huge losses if the range is large. I try to avoid this whipsaw by trying to buy the retracement following the breakout. If you use a system that exclusively buys breakouts, then are forced to go through the retracement, you will suffer through false breakouts. Often, a false breakout can be anticipated by looking at how much the market has broken the old high before retracing. This is what Gann called "false motion." In other words, go through charts and look at how many times the market went through a new high and broke back under the old high. In addition, keep track of the number of days it spent above the old high before breaking back and also how many points it broke out above the old high before breaking back. Look for the minimum moves. This is the "lost motion." Soybeans, for example, have a tendency to break out above old highs by 3 3/4 cents before pulling back. Other things that influence whether a breakout will continue or pull back is the position of the market in terms of price, the number of swings down from the main top, and the seasonals. I should say this is usually the case for commodities. For stocks, one should look at previous downswings combined with retracements and Gann angles to forecast where a market is likely to pull back, too.

Again, 50% is a generally accepted retracement level. You may find in your analysis that certain stocks have their own retracement characteristic.

Q: *To Dave Landry: I liked the article you wrote on retracements, but I'm going to make you retrace this issue. I have found that many stocks offer an ambiguous "significant low." How do you determine in an inexact situation what the significant low is for your starting point in tracing the move and the subsequent retracement of a stock?*

Answered by Dave Landry 2000-07-22

I thought long and hard on how I could describe the way to pick the best significant high and significant low for use in measuring a retracement. The best answer I can come up with, as I wrote in my article, is that these things should be obvious. This may sound like a cop-out, but I think this standard applies to just about any technical-analysis technique. Therefore, when something isn't obvious, you might want to find stocks where that something *is* obvious (or, at least, "more obvious").

Now that didn't answer your question, so I'll let you know what I look for. For an IPO, obviously, the low of the first day of trading often becomes your low (unless, of course, the stock later trades below that low). For all other stocks, you might look for bases from which a large move has occurred, and also for bottoming formations, such as cups, double bottoms, head-and-shoulder bottoms, and so forth. Again, the more obvious the better.

See also, GAPS, page 89.

TRIANGLES

Q: *For Kevin Marder: You have mentioned several times that handles that "wedge" upward are failure-prone. I have at times noticed what people refer to as an "ascending triangle," which is considered a bullish formation. Is the ascending triangle a longer-term formation, and is the wedge pattern a short-term type of pattern? Is the difference found in the size of the OHLC bars? Please clarify.*

Answered by Kevin Marder 2000-12-23
Good question. I believe you are referring to Greg Kuhn's comment on wedging handles. As with any other pattern, the ascending triangle can be found on any time frame. I believe Greg's reference to "wedging" referred to a stock rising on dwindling volume. Note that many ascending triangles become so obvious that the follow-throughs subsequent to their breakouts are not powerful. Most of the volume emerged on the way up prior to the breakout. My experience is that the ascending triangle is better suited for day- and swing traders.

WITCH'S HAT

Q: *Mr. Marder, I recall a few months ago you referred to something called a witch-hat top. Can you explain what this pattern is? Does one use it as a sell or short-sell signal?*

Answered by Kevin Marder 2000-10-14
A witch's hat peak is an infrequent topping pattern that exemplifies speculation at its extreme, most recently appearing in the biotechs as they peaked in March 2000. A stock like Genome Therapeutics (GENE) soared 300% in five weeks before crashing 84% in the next four weeks. Look at the March 7 top in GENE, and you will notice an outside day on rising volume with a 20% top-to-bottom intraday range and a close in the bottom quartile. For an aggressive trader, this is a setup tailor-made for the short side, with the pivot being the March 7 low.

PATTERN-RECOGNITION SOFTWARE

Q: *I would like to buy pattern-scanning software that can recognize the types of patterns that Haggerty, Cooper and Marder talk about. Are there any you can recommend?*

Answered by Eddie Kwong 2000-02-26

First, let me state an important assumption before answering your question. By pattern-scanning software, I assume you mean software that looks for trading set-ups using a combination of price action, volume and/or indicators. For example, a breakout from a three-month cup-and-handle would be one such setup.

That said, the dominant "software" we use is that which resides between the ears. To be sure, everybody uses charting software and basic technical analysis tools in order to narrow the field. But when it comes to recognizing the patterns, we look at charts with our own eyes and recognize patterns through a combination of knowledge and experience. If you read Haggerty's, Cooper's, Boucher's, Marder's and Landry's work and the articles of other traders on the site, you'll often see charts that refer to patterns that have well-defined parameters, but which still have enough subjectivity to defy a purely logical set of rules. Cup-and-handles, distribution and accumulation days, slim-jims, trap-doors, 1-2-3-4s, etc., are the names of some patterns which may seem mechanical at first, but they come with the following baggage:

1. There are often exceptions that don't quite fit the model, but which are worthy of consideration.

2. The patterns always have to be considered in the context of prevailing market conditions.

3. Some of the most powerful patterns, such as cup-and-handles, have a great deal of variation—enough to thwart the design of a computer algorithm.

In addition, there is something subtle and visceral about looking at the price action as opposed to removing oneself from the process by relying on a computer program. Money Manager and TradingMarkets.com contributor Greg Kuhn said it best. He told me he'd spent many years successfully trading by eyeballing charts. Then he began to feel that there had to be an easier way, so he bought a lot of computer software programs that purport to recognize his key patterns. His trading results deteriorated the more he relied on these programs. Realizing this, he went back to his old approach of relying on the ol' noggin and his profitability went to "new highs." Greg says there is often something subtle going on in trading setups that successful traders pick up on. The moral of the story is that the most challenging path to take is to learn the art of pattern recognition, but it is also the most rewarding one.

GLOSSARY

The following terms appear in this book. Even if you are a more advanced trader, you might want to skim this chapter to see how they are defined for purposes of this manual.

Average Directional Movement Index (ADX)—Developed by Welles Wilder, this formula is used to measure the strength of a market but not its direction. The higher the reading, the stronger the trend, regardless if whether it is up or down. It is calculated based on the Positive Directional Movement Index (+DMI) and Minus Directional Movement Index (–DMI).

Bar Chart—Shows the open, high, low and close of a market.

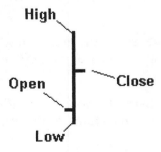

Bow Tie—A trend-following strategy based on the use of a 10-period simple moving average, 20-period exponential moving average, and a 30-period exponential moving average. This strategy relies on the usage of these three moving averages to inform you that the trend has indeed changed.

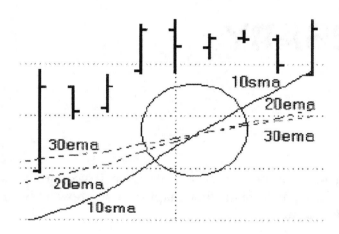

CHADTP—The Connors-Hayward Advance-Decline Trading Pattern (CHADTP) is a proprietary indicator that measures the New York Stock Exchange's (NYSE) advancing-declining issues to identify short- to intermediate-term overbought and oversold conditions in the stock market and the S&P 500 futures. When the CHADTP is above +400, the market is overbought; when the CHADTP is below –400, the market is oversold. Possible reversals are indicated when the indicator ticks down when it is overbought or ticks up when it is oversold.

CANSLIM—Method of stock selection made famous by William O'Neil. Each letter in CANSLIM corresponds to a particular criterion required by the method.

CVR Signals—Created by Larry Connors, Connors VIX Reversal Signals are market-timing signals that use variations of the VIX index to signal short-term tops and bottoms.

Daylight—The space between the low of the bar and the 20-period exponential moving average. Many times, day light signifies that the trend is in place.

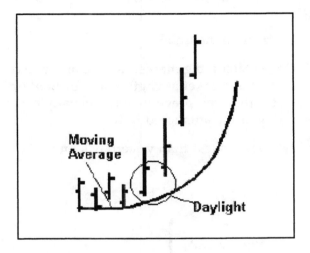

Downtrend—A series of lower lows and lower highs.

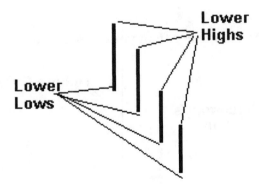

+DMI—see Plus Directional Movement Index.

–DMI—see Minus Directional Movement Index.

Exponential Moving Average—A moving average that gives higher weighting to more recent prices.

Fading—Trading contrary to the trend.

Follow-Through Day—After a big market decline and failed initial rally, a buy setup. A day with unusual market strength (Dow or S&P up 1% or more) and power (volume greater than the previous day), usually occurring between the fourth and seventh day of the attempted rally.

Gap Down—Today's open is less than yesterday's low.

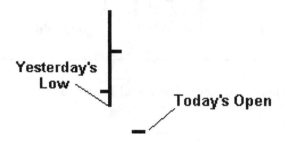

Gap Up—Today's open is greater than yesterday's high.

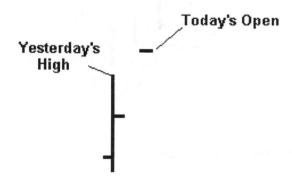

Higher High—Today's high is greater than yesterday's high.

Higher Low—Today's low is greater than yesterday's low.

Historical Volatility—A statistical measurement of how much prices have fluctuated in the past. It can be used to measure risk and potential reward.

Initial Protective Stop—An order placed right after a trade is entered to help control risk.

Lap Down—Today's open is less than yesterday's close, but not less than yesterday's low.

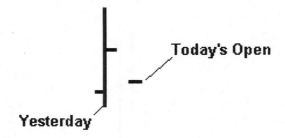

Lap Up—Today's open is greater than yesterday's close, but not greater than yesterday's high.

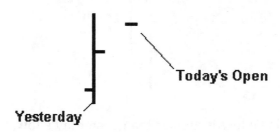

Limit Order—An order to buy or sell at a specified price.

Long—A position that seeks to profit if the market rises. To buy.

Lower High—Today's high is less than yesterday's high.

Lower Low—Today's low is less than yesterday's low.

Market Order—An order to be executed immediately at the asking price for buys and at the bid price for sales.

Minus Directional Movement Index (−DMI)—A component used in the calculation of ADX that measures the downward movement of a market. If it is greater than the Positive Directional Movement, it suggests a downtrend.

Moving Average—The average price of a stock over a given period. For instance, a 10-day moving average would be the sum of those prices divided by 10.

Outside Day—Today's high is *greater than* yesterday's high and today's low is *less than* yesterday's low.

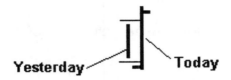

Pivot High—A high surrounded by two *lower* highs. Can also be two equal (or in rare cases three) highs surrounded by two lower highs.

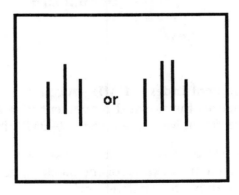

Pivot Low—A low surrounded by two higher lows. Can also be two equal (or in rare cases three equal) lows surrounded by two higher lows.

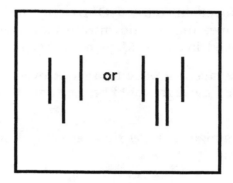

Poor Close—The market closes in the bottom 25% of its range.

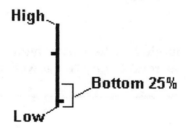

Plus Directional Movement Index (+DMI)—A component used in the calculation of ADX that measures the upward movement of a market. If it is greater than the Negative Directional Movement Index (–DMI), it suggests an uptrend.

Protective Buy Stop—Used to help control losses when shorting stocks. The order is placed *above* the current price of the stock. It becomes a market order if the stock trades at or above the specified price.

Protective Sell Stop—Used to help control losses when buying stocks. The order placed *below* the current price of a stock. It becomes a market order if the stock trades at or below the specified price.

Range—The high price of the day minus the low price of the day. See also, True Range.

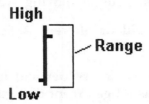

Sell Short—A position that seeks to profit if a market drops in value.

Simple Pullbacks—Three to seven consecutive lower highs after a stock hits a new high.

Stop Order—For buys, an order placed above the current stock price that becomes a market order if the stock trades at or above the order price. For sells, an order placed below the current price of the stock that becomes a market order if the market trades at or below the order price. Stop orders are normally used to help control risk but can also be used to enter positions.

Strong Close—The stock closes within the top 25% of its range.

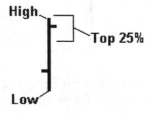

Trend Knock Outs (TKOs)—Trend-following strategy in which one waits for the weak hands to be "knocked out" before entering and trading with the trend.

TRIN—Also known as the Arms Index, the TRIN indicator compares advancing issues/declining issues to the up-volume/down-volume ratio. A reading of less than 1.0 indicates bullish demand, while greater than 1.0 is bearish. The index is often smoothed with a simple moving average.

Triple 9s—100,000 shares bid or offered. A key alert in TradingMarkets' TradersWire.

True Range—Conceived by Welles Wilder and used in the ADX calculation, the true range is the same as range except that gaps (if they exist) are used in the calculation.

True range is the largest value (in absolute terms) of:

1. Today's high and today's low

2. Today's high and yesterday's close

3. Today's low and yesterday's close

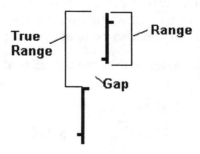

Trailing Stop—A stop adjusted higher for long positions or lower for short positions as the market moves in the favor of the trade. Used to help lock in profits for when the market reverses.

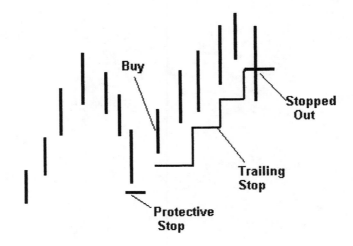

Uptrend—A series of higher highs and higher lows.

VIX—The CBOE Market Volatility Index. It is a measure of the implied volatilities of OEX options.

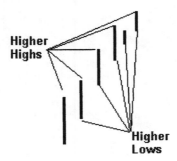

Volatility—How much prices fluctuate over time.

RESOURCES/
RELATED MATERIALS

As I mentioned at the beginning of this book, its emphasis has been to answer questions about strategies that have been explained through other mediums. A complete background and step-by-step instructions on how to apply these strategies is available from their creators in the following resources.

To obtain any of the items listed below, you may go to www.tradersgalleria.com or call 1-888-484-8220 ext 1.

LEWIS BORSELLINO

TradingMarkets2000 Individual Audiocassette –
Trading the S&Ps

Lewis Borsellino is one of the largest and most successful S&P pit traders in the world. Lewis will teach you how to best trade the financial futures indices. He will focus on how to trade trending markets, how to trade range-bound markets, how to use pivot points, how to go long breakouts and fade false breakouts, and how to trade around important economic reports. When you order this tape, you will also receive the special Conference Session Work Booklet to help follow everything presented in this power-packed session.

The Day Trader: From Pit to PC

The subtitle of *The Day Trader, From the Pit to the PC*, indicates the evolution of the trader from floor jockey to computer cowboy. But this is less an account of the trader's changing arena than the story of Lewis Borsellino, a fist-shaking Italian American from Chicago's West Side whose grit and determination helped him become one of the top traders in the Standard & Poor's futures pit.

MARK BOUCHER

The Science of Short-Term Trading

Mark Boucher is a successful trader and money manager. Take advantage of his knowledge and research with his trading course, *The Science of Short-Term Trading*, which includes 500 pages of instruction, eleven 90-minute audiocassettes, CompuTrack and MetaStock user studies, a daily action plan to apply what you learn, and much more.

The Hedge Fund Edge

The Hedge Fund Edge is an indispensable guide for any investor or trader who wants to consistently profit from the markets without having to undergo huge risks. This book provides readers with a solid methodology for achieving market-beating, long-run returns with risk that is substantially below the long-run risk of U.S. and global equities.

TradingMarkets2000 Individual Audiocassette – A Low-Risk Opportunistic Trading Approach to Long/Short Stock Trading

Mark Boucher's hedge fund's performance is known for its consistency and minimal drawdowns. This is because Mark's methodology is to focus on making money both in rising markets and declining markets. In this 90-minute audiotape, Mark will teach you the very best strategies he uses including setups to trade on the long side, his shorting techniques, and his very best intermediate-term market-timing models. When you order this tape, you will also receive the special Conference Session Work Booklet to help follow everything presented in this power-packed session.

JEFF COOPER

Hit and Run Trading: The Short-Term Stock Trader's Bible

Finally, professional stock trader Jeff Cooper reveals how he daytrades and short-term trades the stock market for a living. Among the trading strategies in this book are "Stepping in Front of Size," "1-2-3-4," "Expansion Breakouts," and more.

Hit and Run Trading II

Start making money immediately using the newest techniques and easy-to-master setups. *Hit and Run Trading II* contains: 17 newly revealed trading strategies—readily identifiable patterns you can count on consistently, 22 fully illustrated chapters with 120 sample charts of actual trades, plus answers and insights to the most frequently asked questions about short-term trading.

The 5 Day Momentum Method

Now, for the first time, Jeff Cooper releases the *5 Day Momentum Method,* his most powerful trading system for those traders who are looking for substantial three- to seven-day gains. Rapidly moving momentum stocks always pause before resuming their trend. This book will teach you how to identify the exact day and price to enter these stocks before they explode again. You will usually risk only 1–2 points and your upside potential is 5–20 points, all within five days!

TradingMarkets2000 Individual Audiocassette –
Capturing Profits With Short-Term Patterns

In this 90-minute tape, Jeff Cooper will teach you the exact strategies he uses to trade IPOs, the methods used to make money when the market drops and how he combines multiple time frames to stack the odds in his favor. You'll also learn how Kevin Haggerty and Jeff Cooper constantly adjust trading styles to take advantage of current market conditions. When you order this tape, you will also receive the special Conference Session Work Booklet to help follow everything presented in this power-packed session.

LOREN FLECKENSTEIN

Loren Fleckenstein's How To Trade Hot IPOs

Trading newly minted stocks can produce super-charged returns. If you trade stocks, especially if you trade stocks using chart patterns, you definitely should learn how to fish in these waters. However, the popular image of prodigious riches misses the dangerous flipside of IPOs. This book takes you step-by-step, through three of the best tactics for trading new issues. Each involves chart analysis and deals with trading newly issued stocks *after* they have come public. In other words, these tactics are for those of us who are not among the select few who manage to buy IPO stock at the offering price.

KEVIN HAGGERTY

TradingMarkets2000 Individual Audiocassette – Intraday Trading Tree

Kevin Haggerty, former head of trading at Fidelity Capital Markets, spoke for nearly two hours to a standing-room-only crowd. In this tape Kevin will show you how he selects daily stock setups—how institutions, specialists and market makers think and trade during the first hour—and the best first-hour strategies that enable you to trade on the same side as the professionals. Kevin will show you how to trade opening reversals, trap doors, fading the open, explosive consolidation patterns and how to best trade intraday pullbacks and retracements. The Conference Session Work Booklet is also included when ordering this incredible tape.

Kevin Haggerty's Video Trading Course

How would you like to learn, for the first time, the exact trading techniques Kevin Haggerty uses every day? Kevin recently held an exclusive two-day trading workshop to a sell-out crowd in Florida, and now it's available to you on video. Through Kevin's 200-page trading manual, plus six videotapes, you will be taught the exact methods, techniques and strategies to help you to become an even better trader!

Kevin Haggerty's Five-Week Daytrading Course

If you have followed Kevin Haggerty's daily Pre-Market Opening commentary on TradingMarkets.com over any period of time, you already know how good he is at finding the best daytrading setups day-in and day-out. In this five-part course, he shares with you his knowledge of the markets with a special emphasis on Daytrading. Kevin's course will provide you with the precise knowledge you need to successfully daytrade markets, detailing everything from the type of trading tools you need to how to screen for the best stocks possible to how to exploit institutional movements in chart patterns.

DUKE HEBERLEIN

TradingMarkets2000 Individual Audiocassette – Five Strategies to Maximize Your Profits Using TradersWire

TradingMarkets editors Eddie Kwong and Duke Heberlein show you how to use the up-to-the-second alerts brought to you daily by TradingMarkets.com TradersWire. Intraday breakouts, pullbacks and pivot points are just a few of the dynamic elements covered in this 60-minute tape. A Conference Session Work Booklet is also included when you purchase this tape.

GREG KUHN

Greg Kuhn and Kevin N. Marder's Intermediate-Term Trading Course

Hedge fund manager Greg Kuhn and former Trading-Markets.com Editor-in-Chief Kevin N. Marder teach you the essentials of intermediate-term stock trading in a six-part course. This course will walk you step-by-step through a methodology for entry and exits on intermediate-term trades—trades lasting one week to a couple of months. This is the same methodology used by many of this era's most successful money managers and traders. No theory here, just a solid trading strategy to help you make money trading stocks without having to sit in front of the screen all day.

EDDIE KWONG

The Real Holy Grail: Money Management Techniques of Top Traders

The key to attaining success as a trader is to minimize your losses. In this book, you will receive detailed money-management lessons from the combined wisdom of Jeff Cooper, Mark Boucher, Dave Landry, Kevin Haggerty, and many more experts. This collection of secrets from the world's top traders will teach you how to use different types of orders to get the best possible price and execution, how to place and trail stops, how to manage positions, how to scale in their position, how to adjust position size relative to account size, how to properly use leverage, how to have the discipline to do the right thing, and more.

DAVE LANDRY

Dave Landry on Swing Trading

This book takes you from his daily routine to the exact methods Dave uses day-in and day-out in his own analysis and trading. More than a dozen momentum-based strategies that pinpoint opportunities based on pullbacks and capitalize on false market moves. He also teaches you how to use volatility to select the right stocks and low risk/high reward setups. This is a complete manual on swing trading which includes everything the beginner and intermediate trader needs to get started trading quickly.

TradingMarkets2000 Individual Audiocassette – A Momentum-Based Approach to Swing Trading

In this 90-minute tape, David Landry, Director of Research for TradingMarkets.com and author of *David Landry on Swing Trading,* teaches you some of his best and most successful swing-trading strategies. Included in this dynamic presentation are his strategies he uses for pullbacks, market timing and some of his advanced money-management strategies. A copy of the Conference Session Work Booklet will also be included when you order this tape.

TradingMarkes2000 Videotape Session – A Momentum-Based Approach to Swing Trading

Dave Landry, Director of Research for TradingMarkets.com, will teach you his five best swing-trading strategies. Among the things Dave will teach you are 1) How to enter strong-trending momentum stocks after they've pulled back; 2) How to minimize your risk with proper stop placement while letting your profits run; and 3) Other in-depth methods that you can immediately apply to your trading.

KEVIN N. MARDER

TradingMarkets2000 Individual Audiocassette – How I Trade the Intermediate-Term Trend

Kevin Marder, President of Marder Investment Advisors, shows you during this 90-minute session the exact techniques he uses to identify a large potential intermediate-term stock move. Kevin gives special focus to stock selection, pattern recognition and specific entry and exit points. When ordering this tape, a copy of the Conference Session Work Booklet will also be included.

STERLING TEN

Baker/Ten Electronic Trading Course

This course provides you with what it takes to successfully trade stocks electronically. Through the many trials and tribulations that David Baker and Sterling Ten have experienced in their own trading careers, they have a good idea about what works and what doesn't. Their aim is to provide you with hands-on knowledge that will enable you to sharpen your trading skills. What you won't find in this course is theory; what you will find are practical approaches that have stood the test of time in their own trading.

RELATED MATERIALS

Dave Landry's "Swing Trading Software TradeStation"

Jeff Cooper's *Hit and Run Lessons*

Kevin Haggerty and Jeff Cooper's "TradingMarkets2000 Video—Capturing Profits with Short-Term Patterns"

Kevin Marder and Marc Dupée's *The Best: Conversations With Top Traders*

Larry Connors and Mark Boucher's "Market & Mutual Fund Timing Course"

Mark Boucher's "Hedge Fund Edge Workshop" (Video & Trading Manual)

Mark Boucher's "10-Part Short-Term Trading Course"

Mark Etzkorn's *TradingMarkets.com Guide to Conquering the Markets*

The Best: TradingMarkets.com Conversations With Top Traders

By Kevin N. Marder and Marc Dupee

Dramatically improve your trading results by learning the strategies and techniques of some of the best traders and hedge fund managers in the world. You will learn and absorb how these individuals reached the pinnacle of trading excellence.

Among the things you will learn in this book:

- How **David Kuang** made over $6 million over a six-month period and out-earned Tiger Woods through mid-2000 in his personal account.

- What hedge fund manager **Cedd Moses** does to consistently rank among the top 1% of money managers in the world, according to Money Manager's Verified Ratings.

- Why CNBC calls Lewis Borsellino **"the biggest and the best"** local trader in S&P futures.

- Strategies and techniques from experts: **Kevin Haggerty, Jeff Cooper, David Ryan,** and many more.

A total of 14 interviews where these great traders not only share their life stories but teach you the strategies they use to dominate the industry. **Get straightforward insight to improve your trading results.**

314 PAGES HARDCOVER $29.95

The Real Holy Grail: Money Management Techniques of Top Traders

By Eddie Kwong, Editor-in-Chief, TradingMarkets.com

Have you ever had a stock up 10 points, only to have it turn into a loss in a blink of an eye?

The most crucial factor **to attain success as a trader** is to minimize your losses. Every top trader in the world will tell you that money management is the single most important ingredient. In this book, you will learn important, detailed Money Management lessons from the combined wisdom of **Jeff Cooper, Mark Boucher, Dave Landry, Kevin Haggerty,** and many more experts.

This collection of secrets from the world's Top Traders will teach you: how to use different types of orders to get the best possible price and execution, how to place and trail stops, how to manage positions, how to scale in their position, how to adjust position size relative to account size, how to properly use leverage, how to have the discipline to do the right thing, and more. **If you don't have a way to protect the profits that your trading strategy makes—then there's really no point to trading.**

The strategies and techniques assembled in this book will give you the tools and insight needed to make better trading decisions, ultimately becoming a smarter trader and guaranteeing that all of your hard work finding profitable opportunities doesn't go to waste. **This book is a must for anyone who has the drive to be successful where others have failed.**

136 PAGES SOFTCOVER $45.00

STREET SMARTS
High Probability Short-Term Trading Strategies

LAURENCE A. CONNORS AND LINDA BRADFORD RASCHKE

Published in 1996 and written by Larry Connors and *New Market Wizard* Linda Raschke, this 245-page manual is considered by many to be one of the best books written on trading futures. Twenty-five years of combined trading experience is divulged as you will learn 20 of their best strategies. Among the methods you will be taught are:

- **Swing Trading**—The backbone of Linda's success. Not only will you learn exactly how to swing trade, you will also learn specific advanced techniques never before made public.
- **News**—Among the strategies revealed is an intraday news strategy they use to exploit the herd when the 8:30 A.M. economic reports are released. This strategy will be especially appreciated by bond traders and currency traders.
- **Pattern Recognition**—You will learn some of the best short-term setup patterns available. Larry and Linda will also teach you how they combine these patterns with other strategies to identify explosive moves.
- **ADX**—In our opinion, ADX is one of the most powerful and misunderstood indicators available to traders. Now, for the first time, they reveal a handful of short-term trading strategies they use in conjunction with this terrific indicator.
- **Volatility**—You will learn how to identify markets that are about to explode and how to trade these exciting situations.
- Also, included are chapters on trading the smart money index, trading Crabel, trading gap reversals, a special chapter on professional money management, and many other trading strategies!

245 PAGES HARD COVER $175.00

HIT AND RUN TRADING
The Short-Term Stock Traders' Bible

JEFF COOPER

Written by professional equities trader, Jeff Cooper, this best-selling manual teaches traders how to day-trade and short-term trade stocks. Jeff's strategies identify daily the ideal stocks to trade and point out the exact entry and protective exit point. Most trades risk 1 point or less and last from a few hours to a few days.

Among the strategies taught are:

- Stepping In Front Of Size—You will be taught how to identify when a large institution is desperately attempting to buy or sell a large block of stock. You will then be taught how to step in front of this institution before the stock explodes or implodes. This strategy many times leads to gains from 1/4 point to 4 points within minutes.

- 1-2-3-4s—Rapidly moving stocks tend to pause for a few days before they explode again. You will be taught the three-day setup that consistently triggers solid gains within days.

- Expansion Breakouts—Most breakouts are false! You will learn the one breakout pattern that consistently leads to further gains. This pattern alone is worth the price of the manual.

- Also, you will learn how to trade market explosions (Boomers), how to trade secondary offerings, how to trade Slingshots, and you will learn a number of other profitable strategies that will make you a stronger trader.

160 PAGES HARD COVER $100.00

HIT AND RUN TRADING II
CAPTURING EXPLOSIVE SHORT-TERM MOVES IN STOCKS

JEFF COOPER

212 fact-filled pages of new trading strategies from Jeff Cooper. You will learn the best momentum continuation and reversal strategies to trade. You will also be taught the best day-trading strategies that have allowed Jeff to make his living trading for the past decade. Also included is a special five-chapter bonus section entitled, "Techniques of a Professional Trader" where Jeff teaches you the most important aspects of trading, in-

cluding money management, stop placement, daily preparation, and profit-taking strategies.

If you aspire to become a full-time professional trader, this is the book for you.

212 PAGES HARD COVER $100.00

THE 5-DAY MOMENTUM METHOD

JEFF COOPER

Strongly trending stocks always pause before they resume their move. *The 5-Day Momentum Method* identifies three- to seven-day explosive moves on strongly trending momentum stocks. Highly recommended for traders who are looking for larger than normal short-term gains and who do not want to sit in front of the screen during the day. *The 5-Day Momentum Method* works as well shorting declining stocks as it does buying rising stocks. Also, there is a special section written for option traders.

SOFT COVER $50.00

INVESTMENT SECRETS OF A HEDGE FUND MANAGER
Exploiting the Herd Mentality of the Financial Markets

LAURENCE A. CONNORS AND BLAKE E. HAYWARD

Released in 1995, this top-selling trading book reveals strategies that give you the tools to stand apart from the crowd.

Among the strategies you will learn from this book are:

- **Connors-Hayward Historical Volatility System**—The most powerful chapter in the book, this revolutionary method utilizes historical volatility to pinpoint markets that are ready to explode.

- **News Reversals**—A rule-based strategy to exploit the irrational crowd psychology caused by news events.

- **NDX-SPX**—An early warning signal that uses the NASDAQ 100 Index to anticipate moves in the S&P 500.

- **Globex**—Cutting edge techniques that identify mispricings that regularly occur on the Globex markets.

225 PAGES CLOTH COVER $49.95

CONNORS ON ADVANCED TRADING STRATEGIES
31 Chapters on Beating the Markets

LAURENCE A. CONNORS

Written by Larry Connors, this new book is broken into seven sections; S&P and stock market timing, volatility, new patterns, equities, day-trading, options, and more advanced trading strategies and concepts. Thirty-one chapters of in-depth knowledge to bring you up to the same level of trading as the professionals.

Among the strategies you will learn are:

- **Connors VIX Reversals I, II and III (Chapter 2)**—Three of the most powerful strategies ever revealed. You will learn how the CBOE OEX Volatility Index (VIX) pinpoints short-term highs and lows in the S&Ps and the stock market. The average profit/trade for this method is among the highest Larry has ever released.

- **The 15 Minute ADX Breakout Method (Chapter 20)**— Especially for day-traders! This dynamic method teaches you how to specifically trade the most explosive futures and stocks everyday! This strategy alone is worth the price of the book.

- **Options (Section 5)**—Four chapters and numerous in-depth strategies for trading options. You will learn the strategies used by the best Market Makers and a small handful of professionals to consistently capture options gains!

- **Crash, Burn, and Profit (Chapter 11)**—Huge profits occur when stocks implode. During a recent 12-month period, the Crash, Burn and Profit strategy shorted Centennial Technologies at 49 1/8; six weeks later it was at 2 1/2! It shorted Diana Corp. at 67 3/8; a few months later it collapsed to 4 3/8! It recently shorted Fine Host at 35; eight weeks later the stock was halted from trading at 10! This strategy will be an even bigger bonanza for you in a bear market.

- **Advanced Volatility Strategies (Section 2)**—Numerous, never-before revealed strategies and concepts using volatility to identify markets immediately before they explode.

- and much, much more!

259 PAGES HARD COVER $150.00

About the Editor

Eddie Kwong is the Editor-in-Chief for TradingMarkets.com. Mr. Kwong's involvement in the financial markets began when he and a high school friend became fascinated with the stock market during the late '70s.

Reading numerous books and attending many seminars, Mr. Kwong merged his education with his trading experience and found that the key for his success in the markets boiled down to the basics. Basic technical analysis. Basic chart reading. And basic money management. Over the past 25 years of trading, Mr. Kwong's experience in the markets has also extended into software development and teaching. He has spoken numerous times to the American Association of Individual Investors and Omega Tradestation Users Groups and continues to speak at seminars nationwide.